When a Woman Lets Go of the Lies

Cheryl Brodersen

HARVEST HOUSE PUBLISHERS
EUGENE, OREGON

Cover by Koechel Peterson & Associates, Inc., Minneapolis, Minnesota
Cover photo © Pindyurin Vasily / Shutterstock

WHEN A WOMAN LETS GO OF THE LIES
Copyright © 2012 by Cheryl Brodersen
Published by Harvest House Publishers
Eugene, Oregon 97402
www.harvesthousepublishers.com

Library of Congress Cataloging-in-Publication Data

Brodersen, Cheryl, 1960-
When a woman lets go of the lies / Cheryl Brodersen.
p. cm.
ISBN 978-0-7369-4942-2 (pbk.)
ISBN 978-0-7369-4943-9 (eBook)
1. Christian women—Religious life. 2. Self-esteem in women—Religious aspects—Christianity. I. Title.
BV4527.B745 2012
248.8'43—dc23

2011046147

Printed in the United States of America

12 13 14 15 16 17 18 19 20 / BP-GLD / 10 9 8 7 6 5 4 3 2 1

Once again I find myself indebted to Hope Lyda for her vision, patience, and expertise in transforming my earnest warnings into a readable format. She is simply amazing!

I have great appreciation for those at Harvest House who work with me throughout the publishing process. You people are the best!

My daughters, Kristyn and Kelsey, had a great hand in the inspiration behind this manuscript. They are more than conquerors through Christ Jesus!

I want to thank the girls at the Calvary Chapel Bible College in Murrieta, California, who were in my "All About Eve" class. Their honesty, testimonies, and attentive devotion served as the catalyst for writing on this subject. You girls are terrific!

Finally, I am devoted to my precious co-laborers and prayer partners—the Tuesday Girls! They prayed each chapter into a reality. Among these great women, I give special thanks to Kathy Gilbert for her diligence in reading each chapter and offering such great and profound insights. I am very blessed to have friends like you!

My husband, Brian, is always a great source of encouragement. When I think I have nothing to say, he loves to remind me of all I have said. He is truly one of the greatest gifts God has given me.

Finally, and most of all, I thank the Lord Jesus Christ, who is truth incarnate! I thank Him for giving us the Spirit of Truth to lead us into all truth. I thank the Lord Jesus for His continual love for and devotion to each one of us.

Contents

In the Beginning

The sandals weren't a style I'd normally wear, but they were so adorable. They immediately caught my eye.

They looked so tantalizing in the catalog—a catalog I had never looked at, let alone ordered from. But those perfect-for-summer shoes caught my eye. I imagined how they would look with my different summer outfits. This catalog wasn't one I'd ever even considered buying from before. It was just too sensual. So ignoring the urge to let my eyes and imagination linger on those sandals, I tossed the catalog into the trash.

The next day I couldn't get the wedge-heeled rope sandals out of my mind. I pulled the crumpled catalog out of the trash bin and made the fateful call. I gave the woman on the phone my order. She verified my request: "That would be the wedge-heeled rope sandal?" I concurred and gave her my payment information. As I hung up, I thought about how trendy I would look in my new summer shoes. Or so I thought.

A few days later a package arrived in the mail. I quickly opened it up, eager to see my delightful sandals. But I was totally dismayed to discover *undergarments* ten sizes too large for me instead.

I immediately called the company. They apologized and told me to put the clothes back in the packaging and simply pay the return charges. I complied.

At this point I was feeling a bit uncomfortable. I was wondering if those shoes were really worth the hassle—when another shipment of oversized undergarments arrived. This time when I called the company, the customer service representative was argumentative; insisting that I must have placed this order. After giving her my weight, height, and circumference I finally convinced her I had only ordered sandals.

Ignoring the sense of foreboding, I again repackaged the undergarments and paid return postage fees. Two weeks later, a shoebox-shaped package arrived. I was ready to forgive all injustices just to get those sandals on my feet. With great anticipation I tore off the wrapping and opened the box.

Ugh! The shoes in the box were uglier than a homemade bar of soap, as my mom would say. They only slightly resembled the irresistible pair in the photo. They had a distressed look, as if they had been worn before and discarded. I thought maybe they'd look better when I had them on, but as I tried to squeeze my foot into one, I noticed they were two sizes too small! I called the company and let them know I'd be making a final return. I requested that they never send me anything again. Including a catalog!

Have you ever been deceived by something as innocent as a picture in a catalog? The images are shiny, attractive, and very tempting. They are a lot like the forbidden fruit that lured Eve from her normal behavior and better judgment and opened up the world to lies, hurts, shame, and brokenness. Okay, sandals aren't the downfall of society. But when we believe a lie that is packaged and presented so nicely and innocently, we find ourselves justifying our actions. We buy into the lie instead of God's truth and the wisdom of our faith. Then when we try to force our life into that lie, we realize it doesn't fit the heart and purpose of God's design for us.

Have you encountered problems? Chances are that many of your problems stem back to some lie you have bought into.

Most of us are aware of the problems we are experiencing but are much less certain about where those problems came from. Maybe you too have spent many waking hours rehashing and revisiting your emotional hardships in an effort to find their origin and, just maybe, find a remedy. Are you surprised when anger rises up in you during a conversation or the happenings of a regular day? Has jealousy seeped into your thoughts and undermined a relationship? Does a false belief that you aren't any good take over when you are about to start something new?

Our biggest problems seem to make an appearance with clamor and without invitation. And then they accompany us on our journey as if they had been with us since the beginning. I want you to know that there is something to that sensation. These problems, these thought- and energy-consuming issues, are born of the lies that have been a part of the human experience, the female experience, since the very beginning in the Garden of Eden.

Do you feel dissatisfied? Unfulfilled? Betrayed? Insecure? Oppressed? Unloved? Abandoned? Vulnerable? Afraid? Unworthy? Then you are not alone. Some of these feelings might be tied to specific circumstances or particular seasons of your life. Others might be struggles you hold onto or that seem to hold onto you. Either way, it is time to head for the garden. If you and I are going to discover why our problems are our problems, then we must uncover the lies that distort our perspective and purpose. Those lies have been with women since the time of Eden.

Get Rid of What Doesn't Work

On our way to a full and whole life, we will want to have plenty of room in our minds and hearts for what *does* work. God's hope. God's answers. God's promises. God's truths. And here is some great news: We also get to let go of what doesn't work. It will take some soul-searching and might even involve a few painful goodbyes as you bid adieu to behaviors, lies, and patterns that have been a part of your life for a long time. But it will be worth it because you'll be moving toward real answers by looking at the real causes for the problems.

Have you ever sat down to talk about a problem with your husband, a brother, or a male friend and had this experience? You start to explain that something is troubling you. You mention what might have led up to this trouble because it's complex and not easy to state in one sentence or two. Then just as you get comfortable and start to dig into the actual problem, you notice the perplexed look on your male listener's face. And as he opens his mouth, you know beyond a shadow of a doubt that what he is about to say, what he is about to offer up *before* you even fully explain the complexities of your issue, will be a painfully unhelpful suggestion.

Why? Because men think differently than women do.

Men approach situations with the thought of conquering the issue or the problem. Here are examples of the quick fixes a man might offer for our complicated scenarios:

Depression? Try a new exercise.

Hurt? Ignore that person.

Isolation? Join a health club.

Misunderstandings? Ignore it.

Insecurities? Get a new outfit.

Oppression? Get some fresh air.

Unfulfilled longings? Eat a hot-fudge sundae.

Sound familiar?

We don't want a temporary fix to a long-lasting problem. We want to figure out the "why" of a problem. "Why is this happening?" Now, before I spark a debate in marriages, let me state that men often offer us right answers. We know their counsel can be wise, godly, and exactly what we need to hear. But there is a process that most women go through to come to the other side of an answer that is of lasting influence in their lives. To make a change or to resolve an issue, we need to fully understand a few things, including

- how the difficulty is affecting us
- what the actual issue behind the difficulty is
- where the issue or problem came from
- what the absolute right answer to resolution is
- how to let go of the problem
- how to embrace the answer and make it work

When it's listed out like that in black-and-white, it is clear that we have more steps and stages to go through than the first list of quick fixes. Even if these aren't all a part of your personal process, chances are that you recognize a few from your problem-solving kit.

We don't want pat answers. We're women. We're smart, creative, and emotional beings. We want to examine things and understand them. We want to talk through our to-do lists and the things that occupy our thoughts and our occasional sleepless nights. Even when our feelings confuse us or leave us more perplexed about our purpose than ever, we want to talk about them. It is actually a very remarkable and noble trait to want to understand who we are as women and as daughters of the King. This will serve us well in the journey ahead.

Where to Go from Here?

All problems originated a long time ago in what was a delightful paradise. And the woman who faced them first was Eve. Her name means "life-giver" and she is referred to as "mother of all." Each of us bears a strong resemblance emotionally, mentally, and spiritually to this great mother we all share.

To know why we think and feel the emotions we do, it's helpful to go back to the story and life of Eve. As we study her we will begin to understand ourselves and learn how to let go of the lies and grab hold of God's life-changing truths for our own personal journeys.

....

There is great blessing when you embrace the very best purposes and wonders that God has planned for you.

....

"In the beginning" is the start of God's Word and the start of our journey to discover more about our nature, God's nature, and the wonderful new garden path we can walk when we are willing to release the lies and start living in the glorious truth, purpose, and hope our loving Creator intended for us...in the beginning. God longs for us to walk in this life with the wisdom we glean from Eve's story, from the riches of His Word, and from our own personal encounters with the living Christ.

A life of integrity and wholeness takes some work. There is a need to let go of lies and ungodly behaviors that undermine your faith journey. And there is great blessing when you embrace the very best purposes and wonders that God has planned for you. Can there be any sweeter joy and motivation?

To find our way to greater awareness of God's hope and strength, you and I will explore stories from other women and stories and instruction from the Bible. And we'll also mine our personal experiences to discover what is holding us back from embracing the freedom, love, value, hope, and purpose God designed for us.

Part One

Chapter 1

The Conception of Deception

We're smart women. We pray. We care about what God wants for our lives. Right? So why are we still susceptible to the lies that can undermine or destroy our lives emotionally, spiritually, and physically? How is it we can be deceived? Well, just as Eve went against God's instruction and plan for her and Adam by eating of the tree of knowledge of good and evil, we often make choices that let sin into our lives. Though we listen to God, nod, and enjoy our path of purpose, all of a sudden we find ourselves staring longingly at something forbidden or "less than" what He wants for us.

Let's take a look at how we let sin in and also become aware of the places we've already let sin in. It isn't always obvious to us when we are feeding off of the dangling fruit of deception rather than on a steady diet of truth. Others might notice before we do. But eventually the ungodly thoughts and behaviors become apparent. The weight of carrying around the lies makes us weary. The effort we put into pretending all is well takes every bit of our strength and energy until one day we wake up with a fatigue that is bone-deep.

Even if it is a hardship that has brought you to this point of exploration, my friend, I am grateful that you have the courage and desire to examine the lies that might be a part of your past or present. It can take quite a jolt to our version of "life as usual" before we wake up to the deep desire to walk closely and authentically with God. Whatever has brought you to this place—your personal "in the beginning"—consider it a gift because this is a journey that will transform your life.

How Sin Gets In

Sin doesn't just happen. There is usually a deliberation, a turning point that takes place when we go for the behavior, decision, thought, attitude, or action that aims us away from godliness. James 1:14-16 highlights the progression of sin:

> *Each one is tempted when he is drawn away by his own desires and enticed. Then, when desire has conceived, it gives birth to sin; and sin, when it is full-grown, brings forth death. Do not be deceived, my beloved brethren.*

With Eve, sin started with the notion that Satan put in her mind about the tree of the knowledge of good and evil. He put questions in her mind about the relevancy and validity of God's Word. From there he denied the power of God's Word and the consequences of sin. Finally he made false claims concerning why God had forbidden her from eating the fruit of the forbidden tree. He told her that the fruit would actually enhance her life.

It was not a sudden impulse that caused Eve to pick the fruit off the tree of the knowledge of good and evil. There were forethought and deliberation in her actions. Genesis 3:6 records those deliberations: "When the woman saw that the tree was good for food, that it was pleasant to the eyes, and a tree desirable to make one wise, she took of its fruit and ate."

There was a progression to Eve's actions. First her attention was drawn to the forbidden after a conversation with the devil. Next, she began to look at the tree of the knowledge of good and evil differently. She thought about the flavor of the fruit—"it was good for food." She tried to imagine the taste of the fruit of the tree. She longed for the sensation of biting into the texture of the objects hanging from the branches. She dreamed about taking in what God had prohibited.

Eve felt an attraction to the tree. "It was pleasant to the eyes." She found herself irresistibly drawn to the middle of the garden, where the tree was planted. She stared longingly at the beauty of its shape, branches, leaves, and succulent fruit.

She began to speculate about what would happen to her if she ate the fruit. "Desirable to make one wise"—what would it be like to be wise? Eve, who had felt perfectly content before, now felt like her life lacked something vital. She felt incomplete. The other trees could not compensate for what she felt was missing in her life. The wisdom she already possessed was no longer enough. All her hopes, desires, and aspirations became centered on the tree of the knowledge of good and evil.

The account in Genesis does not tell us how long Eve thought about the tree. She might have thought about the tree for a few minutes, hours, days, or even weeks. The fruit on the tree began to push out every other thought. She might have envisioned it in her mind when she closed her eyes. She might have dreamed about it while she slept.

The tree that hadn't been a big concern for her before suddenly became prominent in her thoughts. She was allowing it to become bigger and more important than God's instruction and the truth she had been experiencing since her creation—that God had given her all she needed.

Healthy Desires vs. Destructive Desires

Sin begins with desire. But before we talk about the slippery slope of ungodly desire, I want to make it clear that not all desire is evil. In fact most desires are not evil. God understands desire. In Psalm 37:4, God promises that if we delight ourselves in Him, He will give us the desires of our heart.

As women we desire many good things. We desire…

- companionship
- love
- acceptance
- affirmation
- fulfillment
- purpose
- meaning
- identity

- food
- pleasure
- happiness
- health
- beauty
- security
- fun
- self-enhancement

Sometimes a good desire is twisted into a bad desire. Satan is a master at perversion. I will never forget the time a woman at a retreat confessed to me that she was in love with my husband, Brian. After all, who could forget a conversation like that!

Believe it or not, I looked at her with compassion. She was a new Christian and had only been attending our church for a short time. Her husband was not a Christian, and he had a problem with alcohol. I knew she had brokenness and sorrow in her life. I also knew, as soon as the words left her mouth, that she was speaking a lie.

Does this mean that I think that she was intending to lie? No. But I recognized that she was speaking from a deception she had embraced as truth. So I kept my composure and my compassion and spoke truth to her.

"You're not in love with my husband. You are in love with Jesus in my husband," I told her.

She shook her head. "No. I think about your husband all the time, and I have had some perverse dreams about him."

This new scenario required a little more grace on my part, but God let me see the truer picture. "Satan is trying to pervert something precious and pure. You are falling in love with Jesus, and Brian is the one who is telling you about Jesus. You think you are in love with the vessel, but really you are in love with the Lord."

I prayed with her and assured her of my forgiveness. Later that year her husband got saved, and their marriage and life took a dramatic upward turn. She was embarrassed that she had once thought she was in love with her pastor. She came to understand that Satan had wanted to keep her from the true desire of her heart and her true path.

Innocent Beginnings

Desire might start innocently in the mind. Then the devil comes along and begins to suggest to you that you need to fulfill the desire for yourself. He might tell you that God doesn't care about fulfilling your desires. He might say that God won't ever fulfill it. Or he might suggest that God is taking too long to fulfill it. Satan will recommend ways to fulfill it on your own. His voice will have a sense of urgency, and you'll feel pressure to move forward in your strength and direction rather than in God's strength and perfect will. How often have you grabbed at the first opportunity that came along and realized you had done so to fill the void and because you were unwilling to wait for God's best?

When a desire becomes your only focus and interest, so much so that you are willing to sacrifice God's ways and plan to fulfill your longing, you are entering dangerous territory. Eve provides us with an example of a woman who stopped heeding God's Word for her life. Her desire to taste something new, hold something beautiful, and to be "wise" was not evil, but because she wanted them on her terms and in her own timing rather than in the ways God planned to usher them into her life, she undermined her commitment to Him.

Taken by Surprise

Eve was unaware of the serpent's real identity and nature. She never thought she would come across something bad in the Lord's garden. And she didn't have a concept of evil. Although we have years of personal history and also the wisdom of Scripture to give us more insight, we can still be unaware and caught off guard by the presence of evil, sin, and temptation when we don't guard our hearts with God's truths and promises. We don't think we're entertaining the devil because we don't expect to find him in our home, our situations, and our sacred places. "Be sober, be vigilant; because your adversary the devil walks about like a roaring lion, seeking whom he may devour" (1 Peter 5:8). He can be found just about anywhere...a truth we discover in our day-to-day lives. Be aware that Satan could be lurking anywhere, ready to deceive you.

Darla's Downfall

Darla is a beautiful woman. She has fiery brown eyes and sculpted features. She met a young man at her father's church. At first their relationship was wonderful. He constantly flattered her and endeared himself to her with gifts. However, after a year or so of dating, he began to pressure her into immoral activity. The pressure intensified and he took more control of her mind through constant criticism and by withholding approval. For years she was in bondage to the relationship with this man she had met at church. One day, at a Christian women's retreat, the reality of this young man's nature dawned on Darla. With the help and prayers of family and friends she ended the relationship. She now refers to those years as the years she dated Satan.

We come to church to worship our Lord and to bring our
brokenness before Him. If we lose sight of this truth,
we place our attention on the wrong things.

Darla never expected to meet someone ungodly at her father's
church. The church would seem to be the safest place to meet a
promising, righteous young man. He came to services, carried a
Bible, and acted like other Christians. In the beginning he was
full of flattery and offered her security and fulfillment. Though in
retrospect Darla says she saw early indications of his controlling,
angry nature, yet she thought she could handle it. After all, she
had met him at church. Sadly, she let desire override her discernment of God's truth.

When we let a longing for love and companionship take over
our hearts, we crowd out God's leading. We drown out the still,
small voice calling us to truth. If we are honest with ourselves, we
even try to ignore the loud calls of conviction because we want
what we want at the time, and we think we know best.

Darla thought the physical garden of church would be a place
where she could give herself over to her desires and it would all
be good with God. Haven't you heard? The church is indeed the
body of Christ, but it is also made up of very fallible humans. We
come to church to worship our Lord and to bring our brokenness
before Him. If we lose sight of this truth, we place our attention
on the wrong things.

The Garden of the Mind and Heart

It is not only physical places Satan has access to, but also to our
minds. Satan tries to enter our thoughts. He introduces thoughts,
fictional scenarios, and lies.

When my friend Nancy was going through a particularly

difficult time she commented to me, "I can't afford to think my own thoughts." Nancy was well aware of the warfare that was taking place in her mind. She couldn't trust every thought that came to her. She had to discern what was true and what was being suggested to her.

There is biblical evidence for this reality. In Matthew 16 Jesus asks the disciples, "Who do you say that I am?" Peter answers with a wonderful disclosure about the true nature of Jesus when he states, "You are the Christ, the Son of the living God" (Matthew 16:15-16).

Jesus responds to Peter's disclosure by telling Peter that this declaration was a divine revelation. "Flesh and blood has not revealed this to you, but My Father who is in heaven" (verse 17). Peter did not naturally come up with this divine disclosure. God had given this revelation to him. However, just a short time later, as Jesus was talking about the suffering He would endure in Jerusalem, Peter rebuked Him: "Far be it from You, Lord; this shall not happen to You!" (verse 22). No doubt Peter felt he was on a roll, having had his last utterance identified as divine. However, this time, Jesus' reaction is quite different. "He turned and said to Peter, 'Get behind Me, Satan! You are an offense to Me, for you are not mindful of the things of God, but the things of men'" (verse 23).

How could it be possible for Peter one moment to have a divine revelation and the next to have a satanic one? Satan intruded into his thoughts.

Notice how Jesus identified Satan's activity. He stated that Satan was mindful of the things of men above the things of God. Satan appeals to the lust of men's flesh. He makes men and women think about what pleases them. This will help you with your own thoughts. Thoughts that center on self-pleasing rather than on God-pleasing need to be carefully examined.

Settling for Less than God's Best

At the inception of desire, it's important to ask the Lord to clarify what it is you really want or should want. Ask for His will to become known before Satan begins to twist the desire in your mind. There are times when God will put a desire in our hearts because He is preparing to give us something special. Paul talks about God working in us to will and to do for His good pleasure (Philippians 2:13). Satan seeks to corrupt the desire so that we will not wait for the greater gift from God or recognize it when it comes.

King David was walking on his rooftop one evening when he saw a beautiful woman bathing near his palace. Her name was Bathsheba, and she was the wife of one of his best soldiers, Uriah. David had her brought to him, and the result was disastrous.

A few weeks later Bathsheba sent a message to David informing him that she was pregnant with his child. The king decided to try to cover his sin. He brought Uriah back from the battle under the pretext of wanting information about the army of Israel. David spoke to him and then sent him home to spend the night with his wife.

Uriah didn't cooperate with David's plan. Being a true soldier, Uriah thought about the other men on the battlefield. He felt guilty sleeping in his cozy bed with his beautiful wife when his comrades were sleeping in the open fields away from the comforts of home. He made his bed that night near the entrance of David's palace, along with the other servants.

David was dismayed. He tried one more time—he wined and dined Uriah and got him drunk. Again Uriah refused to go to the comforts of his own home.

David then sent Uriah back to the battlefield. David instructed his general to put Uriah in the front of the battle and then draw the troops away from him so that he would be killed. After Uriah died in battle, David took Bathsheba into his house and made her his wife. Everything seemed concealed until the king received a visit from Nathan, the prophet.

Nathan began by telling the king the story of a rich man who had stolen his neighbor's only sheep. David was enraged at the rich man and ordered his death. Nathan then said to David, "You are the man!"

The prophet delivered this message from the Lord:

> *Thus says the LORD God of Israel: "I anointed you king over Israel, and I delivered you from the hand of Saul. I gave you your master's house and your master's wives into your keeping, and gave you the house of Israel and Judah. And if that had been too little, I also would have given you much more!" (2 Samuel 12:7-8).*

God had done so much for David already and was prepared to do even more for him. But David had sinned by taking what he desired instead of abiding by the Lord's leading. David, in fulfilling his own desires, had settled for much less than what God had planned for him.

Before the Fall

Corey, a woman with Alzheimer's, came to visit me. Conversing with her for very long proved challenging, so I decided a simple distraction might be best. I turned the television on and settled on an episode of the old series *Perry Mason*. That seemed a safe choice.

Corey became very quiet and focused. She enjoyed the slow-moving courtroom drama. I was congratulating myself on the good decision, when all of a sudden she jumped to her feet and rushed at the television. "You're lying!" she screamed at the woman in the courtroom scene who had just taken the stand.

She turned to me with desperation in her voice, "We've got to stop her! She's lying."

In vain I tried to convince Corey that the scenario wasn't real. I tried to point out that everything in the room we were sitting in was in vivid colors while the drama on the television was being played out in black-and-white. She sat down resolutely. "I am so angry at that woman," she fumed.

At the time I was so surprised that Corey thought she could actually influence something happening on the screen. Yet, when it comes to the story of Eve in the Bible, I often find myself behaving just like Corey. I enter the drama and as Genesis unfolds, I see Eve's attention focusing on the forbidden fruit. I know what will happen. I know this is the craziest thing this woman in paradise could do. And every part of me wants to call out to her, "Turn away! Think about Adam! Think of future generations of women!"

As Eve walks toward the tempting fruit dangling from the tree, I want to warn her with every part of my being. "Turn away. Walk away now!" I don't want her to fall from God's grace. I don't want her to follow through with this action that will forever change her relationship to her Creator.

But her hand moves closer to the forbidden fruit until she is holding it in her grasp. She tugs and it falls softly into her hand. She lifts the tantalizing morsel to her mouth. Her lips part and her mouth opens wider to take a bite of the succulent fruit.

"No!" I want to cry out. "Don't do it."

Though I've read this story a thousand times, it always ends the same way. Eve takes that bite and there is no turning back. Her teeth pierce through the skin and into the meat. She savors it for a moment. As she chews the prohibited pleasure, she passes it to Adam and he bites down on it also. The deed is done.

Innocence Lost

It'd be nice if we had someone shouting out a warning when we or a loved one was about to fall. Sometimes the warnings are subtle or nonexistent, and the mistake, the sin, and the consequence happen.

My friend Betty's daughter got involved with a pedophile on the Internet. Carrie thought she was corresponding with a boy her own age. The man portrayed himself online as a peer so that he could entice her to stay in communication. He flattered her, and finally emotionally seduced her. By the time Carrie realized that she was being deceived, she was mesmerized and under the influence of the bond he had created.

Betty found out that the man had seduced her daughter, so she tried to put an end to their communications. However, Carrie would sneak off to a friend's house or to the library and use other computers to keep the conversation going. The man became cruel in his e-mails, but she couldn't distance herself from him or the abuse. She begged for his approval. Finally she could not take the pain and rejection any longer. At 15 years of age she committed suicide.

> When we refuse to acknowledge darkness,
> we forget to cling to the light.

Betty was devastated. Her precious daughter had been told lies about her value. Her daughter had given her bright future over to someone with evil intentions because she believed his deceptions more than she believed the truths she knew about love, grace, and acceptance from her family and God.

Through this time of great pain, Betty felt a growing desire to warn other mothers. I asked her what message she wanted to convey to other moms. Without hesitation, she answered, "Tell them to teach their daughters the value of healthy fear."

Betty explained that she had shielded her daughter from every story about evil men and women. Carrie had grown up believing that everyone and everything was safe. She had no idea that someone would act with malice toward her.

This part of the story is not unique. Many of us try to protect our children and ourselves from evil by avoiding the acknowledgement of evil. We set up boundaries and borders. We might do such a good job of excluding talk of evil that we forget how a foundation of information and healthy awareness can become our best protection against harmful situations and people. When we refuse to acknowledge darkness, we forget to cling to the light.

When anyone pretends that sin and evil are merely dramatic features of the Bible and have nothing to do with life today, they will become very susceptible to falling into patterns of sin and self-deception. Our advance warning is found in the advance preparation of studying God's promises and truths and by becoming aware of evil's existence so that we are never complacent or unbelieving.

Rising to God's Best

Satan is out there lurking in unexpected places. He is waiting and wanting to deceive women into unproductive lives by his lies. Our best defense against his lies is a solid understanding of the truth. Jesus Himself is the truth we need to grab hold of. In John 14:6 He told Thomas, "I am the way, the truth, and the life."

The closer your grow to Jesus and the more you fill your mind and heart with His truth, the less susceptible you will be to the lies Satan would like to feed you. God has great plans and purposes for your life. Satan would like to subvert those divine plans and keep you in bondage to lies.

Together we will explore the lies Satan suggests and the greater truths found in Jesus Christ—the truths that will set us free from those lies and bring us into the greater purposes of God. Are you ready to be set free? Then let's continue!

Questions for Study and Personal Reflection

1. Read the first two chapters of Genesis. What phrases jump out at you? Is there anything you noticed in this reading that you hadn't paid attention to before?

   _____

   _____

   _____

   _____

2. What intrigues you most about Eve? What can you relate to the most in her story?

   _____

   _____

   _____

   _____

3. This is your "in the beginning" opportunity to make some changes.

   What excites you about embracing some godly changes right now?

   _____

_____

_____

_____

What makes you nervous about a new beginning...even a good one?

_____

_____

_____

Why is "right now" an important time to be reading this book?

_____

_____

_____

4. Can you identify any difficulties or struggles in your life right now? What are they?

_____

_____

_____

5. When have you settled for less than God's best? What impact did that decision have?

_____

_____

6. If you were watching your life on instant replay, at what point would you call out to the screen, "Don't do it! Don't do it!" Describe a time when you were deceived or almost deceived by the devil.

_____

_____

_____

7. Pray and ask God to shed light on some areas of deception that are a part of your life. As you read this chapter, were there any warning alarms sounding in your heart and head? Write down those areas of possible concern.

_____

_____

_____

Chapter 2

When We Face the Lies

How can you recognize when you are hearing, believing, or even acting on a lie? After all, one of the characteristics of a lie is its deceptive power. How are we supposed to recognize it? I have found that there are certain symptoms I experience when I'm exposed to a lie. In this chapter we are going to explore some of those symptoms so that you can begin to recognize and confront the lies you have heard or believed.

There are times when I am talking with someone that I overreact to a certain subject. I've also become discouraged in the wake of a conversation that I had had, but I can't discern why. Has that ever happened to you?

I've had days when my mood has spiraled downward and I've ended up in a heap of confusion...sometimes in tears. I have lugged around the baggage of negative emotions and dealt with the havoc they cause for days, weeks, and sometimes even years before taking the time to explore the cause.

Ideally, we'd face the lies and the struggles willingly and sooner rather than later. But how can we learn to do this? Through the exploration of God's truths and the identification of the lies we hold onto, we can learn to pause and pray when we experience a strong reaction to a statement, thought, or event.

Each time you experience the fallout of the lies you believe, it's an invitation to gain greater self-understanding and deeper intimacy with God. Pray and ask Him to reveal to you what is truly bothering you. When you find yourself in a discouraged or agitated state of mind and spirit, ask yourself, "What lie am I believing instead of God's truths? What hurt have I allowed to fester because I didn't want to face it? Which of His truths have I forgotten?"

My friend Teri leads a class for women who are dealing with substance abuse. She was addicted to drugs and alcohol for over 20 years of her life until she met Jesus. She explained to me that women often turn to substances to numb feelings that they can't identify. I could relate to this. I wasn't taking pills or drinking, but I was clearly finding other ways to ignore or "numb" the feelings rather than acknowledge them.

The women who experienced success in their pursuit of sobriety learned to identify those feelings and turn them over to the Lord. When Teri first got sober she was given a journal. Inside the front cover of the journal was a list of different emotions ranging from fear to happiness. Each day when she woke up she was to choose one of those emotions and describe how she was feeling in her journal. She said that was one of the hardest exercises she ever had to do. Why? Because more often than not, she couldn't identify what she was feeling.

> As we explore our feelings, we'll realize they are the *symptoms* of lies that are already deeply rooted in our minds and hearts.

This would be a very helpful exercise for most of us to do because we spend little time making sense of the emotions or pains behind our daily struggles. We don't make it a priority to be still, prayerful, and attentive enough to take inventory of our feelings.

When we are unsure about what's going on inside us, we miss out on the chance to seek God's guidance through our times of pain, frustration, anger, sadness, and other emotions. As a result, we become much more vulnerable to believing lies.

Know that you aren't the only one to experience uncertainty about the source of your emotions. I've learned a lot by talking to other women about the fears and lies that impact them the most. As we explore our feelings, we'll realize they are the *symptoms* of lies that are already deeply rooted in our minds and hearts. Such awareness can lead us to our knees. This is a time of humility, vulnerability, and also freedom in the Lord's grace.

Are you ready?

Symptoms of Deception

Eve's story is a story with a purpose. Her story is my story. Her story is your story. Her story is replayed every day in the life of every woman. God put her story in the very beginning of His sacred book and it is exactly what we need to build a foundation of truth so that we can know His love and grand purposes for our lives—even when we stand in the presence of lies. Let's journey back in time to that ancient garden and study the mother of us all.

We'll discover the symptoms that manifest themselves when we are living our lives or even one area of our lives based on a lie. We can draw connections to what we feel and why we feel the way we do. This will open our minds and hearts so that the light of God's truth can fill the places shadowed by deception. With that light illuminating the whole of our lives, we'll then be able to let go of the lies so that we can embrace a deeper understanding of God and His hope. Your new awareness of the sins and lies that are present in your life will serve you and God as you exchange each one for healing, eternal truths.

Symptom One: Vulnerability

Often the immediate symptom of sin is the overwhelming sense of being vulnerable. Before sin became a part of Eve's time in the garden, she had been perfectly comfortable in her own skin and in her circumstances. I'm sure she enjoyed awakening each day to sunshine and the scent of fragrant flowers. Maybe she napped beneath the strong, leaf-adorned limbs of magnificent trees and savored the gift of feeling protected, loved, and provided for.

This was a time when Eve needed no other covering. You see, she was not dealing with feelings of guilt, shame, and fear. She was not anxious about who she was or what she would become or how life with Adam would unfold. She was living symptom-free because the disease of deception had not yet twisted her thoughts, desires, and dreams.

Then the infamous conversation with the serpent took place, and so did Eve's exposure to deception. Suddenly, after taking a bite of the forbidden fruit, she realized that she was unclothed. Now, having disobeyed the command of God, she knew she was defenseless against the elements. When Eve felt a sudden chill on her body, I wonder if her thoughts turned to how vulnerable she was in that moment and forevermore.

One of the effects of sin is the sense of deficiency. The King James Bible sometimes uses "debt" to describe sin. I think that is an apt definition. Sin takes something away from us and leaves us lacking. Sin not only makes us feel deficient, it makes us indebted.

Eve's nakedness made her feel deficient. She had never felt self-conscious before. She had been perfectly content. However, once her eyes were opened and she realized she was naked, she immediately wanted to cover her body. She felt embarrassed and not able to go before the Lord. She knew that now she was lacking the covering of the ideal life God had prepared for her. Where she'd had perfect freedom, she now had the restriction, pain, and doubt brought about by sin.

Symptom Two: Shame

When Adam and Eve understood their nakedness, they searched for a covering. They tried sewing fig leaves together. I can't imagine what that outfit looked like! We are very used to clothes by now, but isn't it interesting how we still work hard to cover our sin? We'll create elaborate plans or detours to avoid being discovered in our nakedness. Or we'll generate more sin by crafting lies to hide the initial sin. What a mess shame makes!

One summer, while at a conference center, I was up at the main office while Brian was helping down at the property's lake. As I finished up some tasks, the administrator got a call. The line indicator showed that the call was coming from a phone down by the lake. As he answered the phone, his face lit up and a smile spread across his lips. He looked at me and placed the call on speakerphone.

"Yes?" The administrator said in a helpful manner.

"Rod?" I heard a familiar voice on the other end. Well, sort of familiar. It was my husband speaking in a fake English accent as he continued, "We need you to send some of those delicious ice cream bars down to the snack shack at the lake."

"Will do! Anything else for you?" Rod asked, still smiling.

"Yes. Don't tell Cheryl. She thinks I'm on a diet."

Rod looked at me and smiled impishly. "That might be rather hard. She's standing right here."

"Then tell her this isn't me," the familiar voice said before hanging up.

You see? It's hard to admit sin even when we are caught red-handed. It's difficult to be up front about our transgressions even when they are about ice cream. The Adam and Eve in us all try in vain to cover up sin in a variety of ways.

We try to cover sin with

- busyness
- distractions
- television
- fantasies
- hobbies
- good causes
- exercise
- food

And if you are my husband, you try to cover up with a fake accent!

The coverings we choose, like the fig leaves, aren't necessarily bad, but they are inadequate. They are too small. They are too thin. They are too flimsy. And try as we might, they will not cover up the shame and destruction of the lies we're living.

The same holds true for anything we use to try to cover sin. It just won't work. As Moses warned in Numbers 32:23, "Be sure your sin will find you out."

Sin steals our innocence and leaves shame in its place. Sin takes away our trust and leaves disillusionment. Sin robs us of our purity and leaves us with a muddy residue. Sin promises fulfillment and leaves us empty.

Symptom Three: Fear

Before Adam and Eve sinned, they enjoyed their late afternoon walks in the garden with God. However, after they disobeyed His Word they were afraid when they heard the sound of Him walking in the garden.

Adam and God shared the fellowship of naming all the animals. God blessed Adam and Eve with each other. He placed them in His own garden, which He planted. He gave them free access to all His bountiful fruit trees. Before sin there was no sense of dread in their relationship with Him. They knew Him only as a blessing God. There had been no cause for fear.

Sin drastically changed Adam and Eve's perspective of God. No longer did they view Him as a blessing God but as a vengeful God. No longer did they anticipate His presence as a time of blessing but rather now as a time of retribution.

When sin enters our lives it makes God appear wrathful rather than loving. People will often ask, "Why would a God of love judge sinners?" Do you see how sin shifts the view of God's goodness and righteousness from something that is beneficial to mankind to something that is destructive? The problem is not the question men ask, but the perspective of sin from which they ask the question.

Sin keeps us from seeing the destructive quality of sin. We don't understand that we cannot be saved if we do not renounce sin. When we choose sin, we choose the very thing that is destroying our lives and keeping us from intimacy with the Creator. No, a God of love does not send people to hell. People choose hell when they choose sin.

Ultimately sin is disobedience to God. It is crazy for us to expect God to bless us when we refuse to obey Him. Jesus promises the forgiveness of sins to anyone who wants to be free and who longs for a close walk with God.

Symptom 4: Isolation and Separation

After the "apple" incident, Adam and Eve did not present themselves to God for their afternoon walk with Him. Instead, they hid among the trees in the garden when they heard God walking in the garden.

When I was a little girl, I listened with eagerness and anticipation for my dad to arrive home after work. When I heard the door open, I would call out a questioning, "Daddy?" This would be met with a jubilant, loving, "Where's my baby?"

As soon as I heard the sound of his voice, I would drop whatever I was doing and fly as fast as I could to the front door shouting, "Daddy! Daddy! Daddy's home!" I experienced pure delight when he scooped me up in his arms and sang to me.

Dad knew the minute he walked through the door whether I had been a good girl that day or not. If I flew to him, then I had been good. If I stayed in my room, then I was in trouble.

When we seek separation rather than unity, we miss out on knowing God and knowing ourselves fully in His truth.

Ordinarily I was excited for my dad to get home, except on those days when Mom said, "Just wait until your father gets home and I tell him what you've done." On those days I wanted to create a barrier between me and my dad. I'd linger in another room or feign preoccupation with a toy to avoid eye contact. I didn't want to disappoint my dad, and I didn't want to deal with the consequences of my behavior. Separation, at least initially, felt better than the truth.

Lies cause us to want to hide from God's presence. They create a chasm between us and our faith community. Without realizing it, we'll distance ourselves from people who might notice changes or hold us accountable. We'll avoid church and fellowship with other believers and probably neglect prayer. And we'll allow ourselves to become preoccupied with work, activities, and almost anything other than God's Word.

When we seek separation rather than unity, we miss out on knowing God and knowing ourselves fully in His truth. He desires to fellowship with us. First John 1:7 says, "If we walk in the light as He is in the light, we have fellowship with one another, and the blood of Jesus Christ His Son cleanses us from all sin."

What Sin Lets In

Think about one of those commercials that uses soft music and lovely scenes of nature's beauty all the while the narrator extols the benefits of a prescription medication. Do you notice how in the last few seconds of the advertisement the narrator's voice speeds up and confesses all the risks involved with the same medication?

Eve only absorbed the extolling voice, the soothing music, and the deceptive beauty when Satan was tempting her. He never warned her of the consequences of the product he was selling—sin. She was enticed by the possibility of something better than she had. She was so attracted to what she'd been told was off-limits that she didn't think about the consequences; she gave herself over to the immediate desire.

When she bought into the lie and bit into the apple, Eve's life was diminished by her sin, and her sin had far-reaching effects. Whereas she was blessed before sin, now she came under the curse of sin. This curse included multiplied sorrows, pain in childbirth, a desire (desperate craving) for man, a diminished position, and a prolonged enmity between Satan and all women.

Every woman has felt the sting of that curse in some way or another. It is the sting of sin. But there were other consequences. God cursed the ground for man's sake. Rather than the earth producing freely and abundantly, crops would now need to be tended. Sin brought forth thorns and thistles.

The process of death had already begun in Adam and Eve.

Their bodies would return to the dust from which they were created (Genesis 3:19). They were expelled from the garden, and cherubim and a flaming sword were placed at the east entrance of the garden to guard the way to the tree of life (verse 24).

Sin had other consequences as well, played out in the following chapters of Genesis. Sin introduced envy, rebellion, murder, lying, theft, violence, disease, and every other harmful and vile thing you can think of.

Don't let anyone tell you that there are no harmful consequences to sin! The consequences are numerous and far-reaching. There is a philosophy that many people have adopted concerning sin—"I'm not hurting anyone else, so let me be." Not so. Sin's ripple effect impacts all aspects of your life, and it will impact others, God's creation, and your ability to walk in the fulfilling paths of His purpose. Have you ever thought about that? By basing your life in lies, you are leaving behind a legacy of deception instead of God's intention for you. That is far-reaching!

Ready. Set. Let Go.

Whether organized or scattered, many women have an uncanny ability to anticipate and prepare for possible troubles or obstacles. Open our purses and you will find just about everything you need for any eventuality.

Broken nail? We've got nail files.

Sudden rip? We've got a safety pin or a travel sewing kit.

Stain? We have a stain-fighting agent ready.

Need a measurement? There's a measuring tape attached to our key chain.

Flashlight? Yep…we have that too.

Coupons? What store do you need them for? We are ready.

We also have pens, notebooks, mirrors, mints, lip balm, makeup, a brush, and maybe even a toy or two to keep a little one entertained. Is it any wonder our purses get so heavy? We are prepared!

But what do we carry with us that will help us when we uncover the lies that have plagued us and undermined our confidence and faith over the years? What is in our hearts and minds that allows us to sift through what we see, hear, read, and encounter with discernment? We can't toss aside or step out of lies until we understand what truth is.

That is what this exciting journey is all about. You and I are gathering the wisdom, insight, and tools we need so that we can let go of the lies and embrace God's truths.

If your Bible and heart are open, you are well on your way.

Questions for Study and Personal Reflection

1. As you read through the symptoms of deception, did you recognize any as being a part of your life right now? Describe how these symptoms are showing up.

_____

_____

_____

_____

2. Have fear or shame been a part of your past story? If so, how?

_____

_____

_____

_____

_____

3. List the three emotions that you most frequently feel. What
   were your most recent experiences with them? If you've started
   a journal, take time to write about these experiences. What was
   going on at the time? Could you acknowledge emotions in the
   moment or only later? Is this an easy or difficult exercise for
   you?

_____

_____

_____

_____

4. Spend time in prayer about the symptoms of deception and
   sin you are experiencing. Ask God to reveal any areas that you
   might not be paying attention to. What are the areas He is shed-
   ding light on?

_____

_____

_____

_____

5. You are making the choice to exchange deception for truth. What are some ways you can prepare your heart and life for this journey?

_____

_____

_____

_____

_____

Part Two

Chapter 3

Lie: God's Word
Can't Be Believed

We don't have time to review the countless sources that validate the veracity of the Bible (that would take volumes!), but it's important to start this chapter firmly stating that *you can believe the accuracy of God's Word*. Over the years, many people have tried to convince me that the Bible is full of contradictions. Yet, no one is ever able to back up their claim.

The arguments of skeptics are dispelled after deeper exploration of Scripture and of historical documents besides the Bible. For example, ancient Syrian obelisks confirm the accounts of battles Israel fought with other powers. Recognized historians such as Josephus verify events mentioned in the New Testament. Anyone desiring tangible proof of the Bible's preserved accuracy need only look to the incredible archaeological discovery of the Dead Sea Scrolls in 1947. These scrolls, found in a cave in the Qumran region of Israel (near the Dead Sea), gave further credence to the purity of Scripture. Every book of the Old Testament, except for Esther, is represented among the many scrolls that date back to between the second century BC and AD 70—making them the oldest known copies of these sacred texts. Such findings reinforce the accuracy, trustworthiness, and faithfulness of God's mighty Word. And this is only one example!

The Bible is true. Psalm 119:160 states, "The entirety of Your word is truth, and every one of Your righteous judgments endures forever." You can trust the Bible!

Just as the Bible accurately reveals truths about historical events, geographical locations, and cultural details, it presents unwaveringly dependable truths about marriage, children, relationships, emotional healing, spiritual prosperity, heaven and hell, and other essential life issues. The question is, are you ready to live by its proven promises, truths, and delights?

I have talked to women who are very frustrated in their marriages, jobs, and personal lives, yet they don't want to obey what the Bible says. They continue to try to work things out using their own solutions, which fail them every time.

Jenny walked into my office for the umpteenth time and sat limply on the couch, looking at me pleadingly.

"Jenny, I have nothing to say to you. I love you, but your situation is not going to change until you simply obey God and do what His Word is telling you to do."

"I know, I know," she repeated in great frustration. Then she started to replay all her past and current troubles. I had heard them all before many times.

I interrupted her by saying, "I can give you sympathy. I can say, 'You poor thing,' as I have done before, but the bottom line is that you need to obey the Bible. All other talk or decisions will lead you right back to this very same place of discontentment and frustration."

She knew I was telling her the truth. Jenny had knowledge of

God's Word, but she didn't want to follow its instruction for her life. She was afraid to fully trust God to do as He said. In the back of her mind a deceitful voice kept telling her, "If you obey God, everyone is going to take advantage of you. If you give yourself to His way, you'll be let down."

Jenny resisted obedience until the frustrations became too much for her. She was weary and finally decided to surrender to doing it God's way. The change in her countenance was almost immediate. The freedom and transformation was significant. Of course, later she wondered why she had waited so long.

It takes surrendering our resistance, pride, and sometimes our past hurts to give ourselves over to God's leading. Can you list the reasons why you've withheld your complete trust? Those reasons have no strength compared to the power of His mercy, love, and truth.

As we pay close attention to God's Word and trust it, we'll be less vulnerable to the lies we tell ourselves and those that Satan presents in blatant and discreet ways. You are headed for the certainty of God's great freedom.

Satan's Strategy

One of Satan's greatest devices is to cast suspicions on the validity of God's Word and His promises. He does this in a variety of ways. His end goal is to make us doubt not only the authenticity of God's Word, but also the personal application of it. Satan wants you to doubt the promises of God because there is a supernatural power known as faith that is ours when we believe God's Word for us.

Satan planted the seed of deception when he questioned the validity of God's Word. He asked Eve, "Has God indeed said, 'You shall not eat of every tree of the garden'?" In other words, are you sure you heard God right, Eve? Did God really say that or did Adam?

Eve answered, "We may eat the fruit of the trees of the garden; but of the fruit of the tree of the garden which is in the midst of the garden, God has said, 'You shall not eat it, nor shall you touch it, lest you die'" (Genesis 3:2-3).

> As Eve distanced herself slightly from God's actual words,
> she was making space for sin to create a wedge
> between truth and deception.

She didn't have it quite right, though. What God actually said was, "Of every tree of the garden you may freely eat; but of the tree of the knowledge of the good and evil you shall not eat, for in the day that you eat of it you shall surely die."

Eve knew there was a prohibition, but she didn't know God's command inside and out. Her misunderstanding of His Word was part of what led to her downfall.

Not only did she omit God's invitation to "freely eat" of all the trees of the garden, but she also added an extra prohibition. He said, "Don't eat." Eve said, "Don't eat. Don't touch." As Eve distanced herself slightly from God's actual words, she was making space for sin to create a wedge between truth and deception.

Satan's next action was to go beyond questions and to state lies. He directly contradicted God when he said to Eve, "You will not surely die." He planted the seed of doubt right there.

Things haven't changed much since the garden. Satan is still trying to cast doubt on God's commands, promises, and truths. The Word of God is powerful and Satan knows this. Hebrews 4:12 states, "The word of God is living and powerful, and sharper than any two-edged sword, piercing even to the division of soul and spirit, and of joints and marrow, and is a discerner of the thoughts and intents of the heart."

The Word of God strengthens and encourages us. It supplies us with the power to resist sin and the devil and the deceptions. The Bible explains spiritual realities to us and supplies us with encouragement and the directives we need. According to the second epistle of Peter, it is through the knowledge of God that we are equipped for all the things that pertain to life and godliness.

Satan doesn't want us to be spiritually strengthened, because when we are thriving spiritually we pay less attention to the deceptions. There is nothing more disappointing to Satan than a Christian who knows their God and is full of faith in His Word and promises!

Satan employs a variety of methods to spawn doubt in the minds and hearts of women. He attacks the inspiration and the purity of the Scriptures. If you are rightly convinced of their inspiration and purity, he will then try to keep you from claiming their promises.

Prepare a Foundation

To guard ourselves against the lies of the enemy, it's essential that we trust God's Word and also *read* God's Word. How can anyone obey, follow, or respect what they don't know?

Many people live on secondhand knowledge of God's Word. They get all their knowledge of the Bible from hearing others talk about it or preach from it. While it is good that they are applying wisdom they are taught by others, they are missing out on the power and lasting impressions of personal encounters with Scripture. And what if someone is directing them in a way that isn't God's truth? They will not have a foundation of knowledge for comparison.

Then there are others who pick up the Bible and read it only lightly, never taking time to meditate or ask themselves about what they read, what God was speaking to them, or how to live out the godly insights.

These practices can prove lethal when we have an encounter with the devil or with anyone or anything that redirects our steps away from God's absolute best for us. What will we say if the devil entices us to doubt as he did Eve with "Has God indeed said..."? If we don't know the Word of God firsthand we'll get it wrong.

The Word of God is the foundation of our faith. It is the rock that holds us up when we are weary, facing changes, walking through a season of doubt, enduring a journey of pain, or experiencing a time of holding steady. Jesus said in Matthew 7:24-27,

> *Whoever hears these sayings of Mine, and does them, I will liken him to a wise man who built his house on the rock: and the rain descended, the floods came, and the winds blew and beat on the house; and it did not fall, for it was founded on the rock.*
>
> *But everyone who hears these sayings of Mine, and does not do them, will be like a foolish man who built his house on the sand: and the rain descended, the floods came, and the winds blew and beat on that house; and it fell. And great was its fall.*

To be prepared for the storms of life, we must personally know and obey what the Bible says. Faithfulness in this arena leads us to the wonder and power of God's promises.

Claim the Promises

Many of the promises of the Old Testament were made to the nation of Israel. Christians are often slow to claim those promises, fearing that they are for Israel alone. But these promises are ours through Jesus Christ.

God made conditional promises to Israel if they kept His Law. Israel was unable to keep the Law as God intended. But Jesus kept the Law perfectly, as He stated in Matthew 5:17, "Do not think that I came to destroy the Law or the Prophets. I did not come to destroy but to fulfill." Jesus kept the Law exactly as God desired men to keep it. Thus, Jesus became the inheritor of all the promises of God. As it records in 2 Corinthians 1:20, "All the promises of God in Him are Yes, and in Him Amen, to the glory of God through us."

What does that mean to us today? That means that we can lay claim to every promise of the Old Testament through Christ Jesus. The promises of God's protection, peace, strength, and help are all ours as we put our faith and trust in Christ Jesus. In Ephesians 2:12-13, Paul writes, "At that time you were without Christ, being aliens from the commonwealth of Israel and strangers from the covenants of promise, having no hope and without God in the world. But now in Christ Jesus you who once were far off have been brought near by the blood of Christ." Whether your heart has wandered or you have only recently come to know Christ, these are your promises.

Satan would have you believe that you are disqualified from God's goodness. We are hard enough on ourselves—we don't need an extra voice telling us that we aren't worthy, right? In fact, those times when you are certain that you aren't good enough for God's grace, the devil is absolutely delighted. He's probably feeding you a list of your past mistakes as you sit there and wonder how God could ever, ever forgive you—let alone lead you in the way of His promises.

Well, my friend, Jesus qualified you by His perfect obedience to God and by His sacrificial death on the cross. God's love for you is limitless and unconditional. Forget that list of past failings. Turn back to the promises that are laid out for you in Scripture. They are for you.

Peter speaks of these promises in 2 Peter 1:3-4.

His divine power has given to us all things that pertain to life and godliness, through the knowledge of Him who called us by glory and virtue, by which have been given to us exceedingly great and precious promises, that through these you may be partakers of the divine nature.

So when you are reading your Bible and find a promise that speaks directly to your situation, write it down! It's your promise through the work and person of Jesus Christ.

Let Go of Uncertainty—Embrace God's Promises

Psalm 119:160 states, "The entirety of Your word is truth, and every one of Your righteous judgments endures forever." Think of the power of God's Word! The Bible records in Genesis that the whole world was without form and purpose and darkness was upon the face of the earth. Then God spoke to this darkness and said, "Let there be light." Immediately the universe was filled with light.

God spoke again and the earth and the heavens took form. He spoke again and plants and trees bearing seed and fruit emerged. He spoke again and there were stars, planets, and galaxies of all different sizes filling the universe. He spoke again and a variety of creatures filled the oceans, rivers, and seas. He spoke again and birds of all shapes, colors, and features flew through the crystalline sky. He spoke again and lions, bears, giraffes, rhinoceroses, elephants, horses, and a host of other creatures with unique abilities, traits, and appearances began to walk, hop, lumber, and run across the vast plains He planted. All this came to be because God spoke.

Satan would deny the power of that creative and powerful Word of God. He would have you to believe that it will not accomplish what God purposes. Nothing is further from the truth. Isaiah 55:10-11 says,

As the rain comes down, and the snow from heaven, and do not return there, but water the earth, and make it bring forth and bud, that it may give seed to the sower and bread to the eater, so shall My word be that goes forth from my mouth; it shall not return to Me void, but it shall accomplish what I please, and it shall prosper in the thing for which I sent it.

When Satan tells you that you cannot trust the power of God's Word, take a look at the sky, the trees, the plants, the animals, and consider the great power of God's Word in the creation of the world. The power that placed stars in the sky is also the power of God illuminating your life today.

Promises, Promises

You can trust the Bible when it comes to Your salvation through Jesus Christ. You can also trust the Bible as a source to discover and know the many promises of God.

I was driving in the car with a young woman who told me of how God had fulfilled certain promises in her life. A year earlier she had been going through emotional turmoil. She had read the scripture, "Be still and know that I am God" (Psalm 46:10). She felt the Lord prompting her to give Him her emotionally trying situation so He could work it all out. It was a struggle for her to release it entirely to God. On good days she would give it to God. On hard days, she would start to take it back. On the tough days, she would open her journal and write down the promises God had given to her.

Turn your mind and heart from the deception
and toward the certainty of God's promises.

During one of those challenging times, she had come to me and asked me if she could trust what God had spoken to her. My answer must have confused her at first, because I said, "Yes and no. Yes, you can trust God's promise if you do what He is telling you to do. No, you can't expect Him to work through you if you are walking in disobedience."

I gave her the illustration of baking a cake. If I follow the recipe I can have the assurance of a delicious dessert. However, if I decide to omit a step like sifting or beating, or I choose to leave out an ingredient, I can't blame the recipe if the cake is a failure.

"You have to do what God says," I told her. "The promise is fulfilled by our obedience to Him." My words were hard for her to digest at the time, but she listened and complied. A year later she was praising the Lord for the veracity of His promises.

Has God given you a special promise or word concerning a person or situation in your life? Have you then heard an insidious voice in your head asking you, "Did God really say that?" Turn your mind and heart from the deception and toward the certainty of God's promises. Let's look at just a few of His great vows:

1. The blood of Jesus cleanses a man (woman) from every sin (1 John 1:7).

2. Old things are passed away and all things have become new (2 Corinthians 5:17).

3. All things work together for the good of those who love God and are called according to His purposes (Romans 8:28).

4. God will work in me to will and to do of His own good pleasure (Philippians 2:13).

5. Jesus will never leave me or forsake me (Hebrews 13:5).

6. His yoke is easy and His burden is light (Matthew 11:30).

7. To be absent from this body is to be present with the Lord (2 Corinthians 5:8).

8. Greater is He who is in me than he (Satan) who is in the world (1 John 4:4).

9. He is able to keep me from falling (Jude 24).

10. Tribulations are working in me for good (James 1:2-4).

11. God will provide all of my needs according to His riches in glory (Philippians 4:19).

12. God hears us when we pray (1 John 5:14-15).

13. Nothing can separate me from the love of God (Romans 8:35-39).

14. No weapon formed against me can prosper (Isaiah 54:17).

15. God is for you (Psalm 118:6).

When you know the Word of God and trust its validity, you can resist the lies and counter them with His promises. You will have the opportunity to examine many more of His beautiful truths as you continue through each chapter. Be encouraged. You are starting off with nothing less than the assurances of His love and direction. What could be better?

Your first act of letting go has allowed you to hold tightly to God's Word as your light, security, and hope. His promises are real. When you get shaky about what to believe and what not to believe, return to His Word. Better yet, don't ever leave it.

Questions for Study and Personal Reflection

1. What lies has Satan suggested to you concerning the Word of God?

   _____

   _____

   _____

   _____

2. What keeps you, or has kept you, from relying on God's Word and surrendering to His will?

   _____

   _____

   _____

   _____

3. How have you been encouraged to trust God's Word in your lifetime and through this exploration?

   _____

   _____

   _____

   _____

4. Compare Genesis 2:16-17 and Genesis 3:2-3. Why does it matter that there's a difference between what God said and what Eve said?

   _____

_____

_____

_____

5. Describe how it feels to let go of uncertainty. What freedom do
   you experience with this big step?

_____

_____

_____

_____

6. Look over the 15 promises mentioned at the end of this chapter. Which promises do you need to claim? List those out here
   and also why they are so important for you to believe and hold
   onto right now. Pray over these today and in the days ahead
   so that they will be in your heart and mind for the rest of this
   adventure.

_____

_____

_____

_____

Chapter 4

Lie: The Devil Made Me Do It

Years ago there was a comedian on television who was famous for saying, "The devil made me do it." He got a lot of laughs from that phrase. Yet, in essence, this is exactly what Eve told God. "The serpent deceived me, and I ate" (Genesis 3:13).

Although it was true that Eve was lured into eating the forbidden fruit by the serpent, at a certain point she made the conscious decision to abandon God's Word to embrace her own desire.

In John 9, the disciples see a blind man begging and ask Jesus, "Who sinned, this man or his parents, that he was born blind?" The disciples were conditioned to assign blame to someone. Jesus corrected them when He said, "Neither this man nor his parents sinned, but that the works of God should be revealed in him" (John 9:2-3).

We, like the disciples, seem preconditioned or at least eager to blame. We are always ready to accuse another person of causing us to fall or fail. Think of all the lawsuits that are based on someone blaming someone else for their decision. Displacing the responsibility is a way that we keep ourselves stuck in a mode of deception. However, when we begin to acknowledge responsibility and the power of God to transform us, we are able to step into the light of truth.

The Blame Game

Blame has become such a common practice in our society that we hardly even realize how often we do it. We blame traffic for making us late to work. (It has nothing to do with the fact we slept in.) We blame fast food for making us fat and unhealthy (as if fast food were forced upon us). We blame the television for wasting our time (but who turned it on?). We blame anyone and everything but ourselves.

Blame is a big lie we buy into so we can avoid the sometimes painful process of acceptance and restoration. Truth doesn't happen if you are pointing a finger at everyone and everything except yourself and your actions Now, I know hard times happen. We face many struggles and heartbreaks that are not of our own doing; however, we experience numerous troubles that we are at least partially responsible for.

While you might not go around saying, "The devil made me do it," I would guess that you have had times of placing blame on others or on a situation for how *you* respond. Delegating blame to others can become one of the biggest lies in women's lives. It can also become one of the hardest ones to let go of.

Let this be an encouragement to you if, as we progress through this chapter, you feel conviction about this lie. As I said, this happens to be a very common problem for many of us. The good news is that there is remarkable relief and freedom when the light of truth is shed on this particular deception. So if you feel challenged, scared, or resistant, remember that those emotions can be symptoms of deeply rooted lies. It's often hard to accept the blame for our choices and actions. However, when we take responsibility for what we have done, we enter the great light of truth.

Don't be afraid. Keep going. Pray. Talk to a friend about going through this book and this chapter with you. Don't let your pride or fear keep you from one of the most transforming experiences you can have as a woman of truth.

The Easy Scapegoat

While we lived in England, Brian purchased an old Volvo sedan to get us around town. That old car sputtered and muttered but faithfully got us everywhere we needed to be from Monday to Saturday. However, without fail, that crazy car would not start on Sundays when we needed to drive the family to church. We finally had to call a mechanic (in England they come to your house!). As Brian and the mechanic, Jeff, talked, Brian shared that he was a pastor of a church in central London. Upon hearing this, Jeff started asking a lot of questions including the question that many have asked through the ages: "How could a God of love allow suffering and pain?" Brian explained to him how sin entered the world through the garden by man's choice to disobey God. "Pain and suffering are the natural consequence of sin but not God's intention for His creation."

> Standing before God as blameless through Christ is a much better scenario than standing before God blaming everyone but yourself for your actions.

Jeff nodded as the reality of what Brian was saying made sense. "So, it all comes down to Eve eating that apple, right?"

Jeff got part of it right. Sin entered the world through Eve's act of disobedience, but I get awfully tired of Eve taking the rap for the world's sin. Just as we can't blame the devil for our actions and decisions, we also can't cast the burden on Eve when we say yes to a temptation. We can't shrug off our responsibility. It isn't easy to stand in truth and for truth. But standing before God as blameless through Christ is a much better scenario than standing before God blaming everyone but yourself for your actions.

What Eve Didn't Know

I once heard a speaker denounce Eve for dialoging with the devil. There is only one problem with this denunciation—Eve did not know she was talking to the devil.

Eve was an innocent. She never expected an evil intruder to come into the garden of the Lord. She felt safe and protected in God's garden. She was surrounded by His creation. She had Adam for a companion. She even walked in fellowship with God in the cool of every evening.

Satan came into the garden as a beguiling creature. The Bible records that "the serpent was more cunning than any beast of the field which the LORD God had made" (Genesis 3:1). Satan was deceptive and disguised. I'm sure that if he had come to Eve in a red suit and a pitchfork in his hand and announced, "Hello, I am here to deceive you and get you to sin against God and bring disastrous consequences to His creation because of my personal ambition and rebellion toward Him," Eve would have refused to give him an audience.

Eve did not know about evil, and because she didn't understand it she was deceived by the devil and became the instrument by which evil entered the world. Think about the following:

- Eve acted in ignorance when she spoke with the serpent.

- She didn't expect someone like Satan to enter into the garden of the Lord.

- She was deceived by the devil's innocent appearance.

- She had no concept of evil.

We, as her descendants, have a definite advantage. We have the knowledge of evil, and by our choice to receive, believe in, and obey Jesus, we can bring life and hope into a dark world. This advantage also means we have more responsibility. We have tools Eve didn't have to recognize lies and make right choices. We are even more culpable for the choices we make. It's time to take responsibility.

What's with All the Questions!

The first time Adam and Eve hear God walking in the garden after they have sinned, they hide among the trees. God calls out to Adam, "Where are you?"

Adam answers, saying he was afraid when he heard God's voice because he was naked. God then asks Adam, "Who told you that you were naked? Have you eaten from the tree which I commanded you that you should not eat?" (Genesis 3:9-11).

God, being omniscient, must have known already what took place in the garden. So why did He question the man?

Throughout the Scriptures we find God asking questions. The reason for the questions is not so He can gain information, but to cause self-reflection and give a person an opportunity for confession. God was giving Adam the opportunity to do the right thing after the wrong thing.

Examining ourselves is a great way to learn from our mistakes. But Adam wasn't up on how to let go of the lies. In fact, he seemed to be very ready to jump on the bandwagon of blame.

Adam said, "The woman whom You gave to be with me, she gave me of the tree, and I ate" (Genesis 3:12).

Oh my.

Adam ultimately blamed God for his sin. In effect he was saying,

"God, if You hadn't created and given me Eve, none of this would ever have happened!" It is so much easier to blame Him for everything than to take any personal responsibility. We've explored how detrimental it is to always blame the devil or Eve or another person. Let's take a moment to understand why it is especially harmful and disastrous to blame God for the times we are weak and give in to the invitation to sin.

A young wife I know was struggling with some pretty serious sin. Instead of confessing it as sin and then refusing to give in to it, the woman rationalized, "If God didn't want me to feel and act this way, than He would have taken the desire away."

When we turn it all back on God, we are trying to rationalize our sin. Like the young wife, we say, "Well, God should have taken away the desire." Or "God should have stopped me from acting on my desire."

God does not keep us from sin. He allows us to make choices, even bad choices, so that we might see the inclination of our fallen nature, and call out to Him to help and save us from the evil propensities of our nature. He often allows us to come to the end of our ways so we might ultimately realize our need for Him. Proverbs 16:25 says, "There is a way that seems right to a man, but its end is the way of death." God doesn't want to force His will upon us. He wants us to see the goodness of His will and choose it instead of our destructive desires.

By allowing desire to remain, God allows us the opportunity to deny ourselves, take up our cross, and follow Jesus (Matthew 16:24). We learn to take authority over sin, rather than letting sin take authority over us.

James makes it clear in James 1:13 that God does not tempt people. Sin is not God's fault. "Let no one say when he is tempted, 'I am tempted by God,' for God cannot be tempted by evil, nor does He Himself tempt anyone."

In blaming God, Adam was depreciating the gift God gave him in Eve. And, ultimately, he was refusing to grow and return to a right relationship with Him in that moment. He was scared, stubborn, and silent about his responsibility. Before we get too self-righteous in our perspective of Adam, let's think of times when we've done the same thing. What do you need to get right with God about? What questions do you need to ask or be asked so that you'll examine your life?

We all, like Adam and Eve, make bad choices. However, when we own up to those choices by confessing our sin, God is faithful and just not only to forgive us but to cleanse us (1 John 1:9). Without confession there can be no cleansing, freedom, or restoration.

This journey is about examining the times we are living in lies rather than in the light of God's truth. We'll realize that even with our knowledge of Eve's great folly and Adam's avoidance of responsibility, we've made some pretty substantial mistakes. Ask the Lord to help you to recognize Satan and his evil wherever and whenever he shows up.

Let Go of Blame—Embrace Responsibility

Eve wasn't the only one to have a dialog with the devil. Jesus also had an encounter with him. Unlike Eve, Jesus did not meet up with Satan in a beautiful garden but in the desolate wilderness.

He had been fasting for 40 days and nights when the devil approached him. Satan appealed to His desire for food. "If You are the Son of God, command that these stones become bread" (Matthew 4:3). In effect, Satan was saying to Jesus, "You are hungry. Fulfill Yourself. You, as the Son of God, have the power to do so."

Jesus made a different choice than Eve. Jesus said to Satan, "Man shall not live by bread alone, but by every word that proceeds from of the mouth of God" (Matthew 4:4). Jesus chose the directives of God over His desire for food. Eve, on the other hand, was not hungry. She could eat freely of the other trees in the garden. But she chose to disobey God's Word in order to eat of the forbidden tree because it was in her power to do so. Jesus refused to disobey the Word of God, choosing deprivation over disobedience to the Word.

Eve desired fulfillment from the fruit of the tree. She wanted her eyes to be open so that she could become like God. The devil was eager for her to believe that was possible.

Jesus desired to redeem the world. Satan, knowing that the ultimate objective of Jesus was to rule the world, offered Him all its kingdoms. "All this authority I will give You, and their glory; for this has been delivered to me, and I give it to whomever I wish" (Luke 4:6). Do you see how crafty this is? Satan offers Jesus the fulfillment of His objective without the pain of the cross.

Jesus refused Satan's means to fulfillment. Jesus said, "Get behind Me, Satan! For it is written, 'You shall worship the LORD your God, and Him only you shall serve'" (Luke 4:8). Jesus refused to take the quickest route offered to a desired end. He refused self-ambition. Jesus chose to have His objective accomplished by God alone and in God's way.

Satan made one last attempt. He took Jesus to the highest point of the temple. Then he said, "If You are the Son of God, throw Yourself down from here. For it is written: 'He shall give His angels charge over You, to keep You,' and, 'In their hands they shall bear you up, lest you dash your foot against a stone'" (Luke 4:9-11).

Satan tempted both Eve and Jesus with immediate fulfillment. Eve was all for the possibility of quick power and understanding. In that moment, she didn't care what God's big picture was, and so she took the bait. Her sin wasn't to speak with the serpent, but her decision to disobey God was the downfall.

Satan really played up the potential for immediate power and fulfillment when tempting Jesus. He gave quite a sales pitch, saying that Jesus didn't have to wait on God's timing. Jesus could force God to prove His Kingship to the world right then and there. All Jesus needed to do was to throw Himself off of the pinnacle of the temple in the sight of a large Jewish crowd that would be gathered there. When the angels came to save Him, then the people would have to acknowledge His divinity.

Jesus declined. "It has been said, 'You shall not tempt the Lord your God'" (Luke 4:12). He refused to try to make God amend His timing. He would not attempt to force Him to move before the time was right.

Jesus honored the Word of God more than His desire, His objective, and the immediacy of fulfilling His objectives. He was willing to wait in order that God's Word might be obeyed. This is how He rebuffed the devil.

We can resist the temptations of the devil in the same way Jesus did. When our foremost desire is to obey God's Word and His plan for us, we will not give selfish ambition a foothold.

The promise of James 4:7 is true, "Resist the devil and he will flee from you."

We Miss the Point When We Point the Finger

I had a girl approach me after one of the classes I teach at the Calvary Chapel Bible College. She was upset with the boys at the school for complaining about the way the girls dressed. "I think they want us to wear burkas. What about the way they dress? I think they should have a dress code too!"

When we "get vertical" and see ourselves answering to God and following the example of Jesus, our lives will be made right by His standard.

I told her that I felt the problem was not the way the girls or guys dressed but with the fact that no one was taking personal responsibility for their own issues with lust. "If you have a lust problem, then a woman can be wearing a burka and the guy is still going to lust. In the same way, if you have a guy issue, then it doesn't matter how they dress or what they say, you are going to read something into every gesture a guy makes. It's time for everyone to stop looking at everybody else and get their own heart right before God." Yes, modesty is important. But the point I wanted to make was that every man and every woman is responsible for how they deal with their lust.

A dear friend of mine calls this the "horizontal problem." When Christians start looking sideways at what other believers are doing so that they can rationalize their own actions, they're going to end up with some big problems. However, when we "get vertical" and see ourselves answering to God and following the example of Jesus, our lives will be made right by His standard.

Remove the Blockage of Blame

Shifting responsibility to others can foster an attitude of unforgiveness. Unforgiveness can keep us from the glory of answered prayer. Jesus warned against this attitude in Mark 11:24-25,

> *I say to you, whatever things you ask when you pray, believe that you receive them, and you will have them. And whenever you stand praying, if you have anything against anyone, forgive him, that your Father in heaven may also forgive you your trespasses.*

Taking responsibility for your own actions will lead you to readily forgive. You don't have anything to hold over someone. You made the conscious decision and no one forced you to do it. Therefore, the issue is between you and God. When you and I bring this type of humbleness to prayer, God listens. The psalmist wrote, "LORD, You have heard the desire of the humble; You will prepare their heart; You will cause Your ear to hear" (Psalm 10:17).

God promises to answer the prayer of the people if they will stop blaming others. It says in Isaiah 58:9, "Then you shall call, and the LORD will answer; you shall cry, and He will say, 'Here I am.' If you take away the yoke from your midst, the pointing of the finger, and speaking wickedness..."

Pointing the finger at others keeps us from the power of answered prayer. Have you ever thought about it this way before? Blame causes division. Blame hurts. But taking personal responsibility keeps "the unity of the Spirit in the bond of peace" (Ephesians 4:3). When we are more aware of what we do to others than what they are doing to us, our vertical perspective toward God is in place.

When we blame others, we miss the "all things" aspect of Romans 8:28. Paul emphatically states, "All things work together for good to those who love God, to those who are the called according to His purpose."

God can use pain, sorrow, folly, and even wrong turns to work together for good in our lives. He can take even the worst that happens and use it for beneficial purposes. Some of those purposes include rewards in heaven. Paul also wrote in 2 Corinthians 4:17 that "our light affliction, which is but for a moment, is working for us a far more exceeding and eternal weight of glory."

Not only does God work everything for good on earth, but He uses the things that happen to us for eternal rewards.

If our eyes are busy searching the horizon for someone to serve as a scapegoat for our own behaviors, then we are unable to look to God and ask what He wants of us in the circumstance. He uses confession in our lives. It becomes an act of humility and transformation, and He will work a host of great things into our lives when we let go of the lies we tell ourselves and Him and come clean before Him.

How Confession Helps

Paul highlighted the divine virtues of confession in 2 Corinthians 7:10-11.

> *Godly sorrow produces repentance leading to salvation, not to be regretted; but the sorrow of the world produces death. For observe this very thing, that you sorrowed in a godly manner: What diligence it produced in you, what clearing of yourselves, what indignation, what fear, what vehement desire, what zeal, what vindication! In all things you proved yourselves to be clear in this matter.*

A sincere acknowledgment of our sin unattached to any blame of others produces diligence. Diligence is carefulness in our actions. Diligence causes us to be on guard and take the right precautions. Confession brings a "clearing of ourselves." That "clearing of ourselves" leads to fresh starts and new beginnings.

Indignation against sin also results from the acknowledgment of our guilt. Have you ever been mad at yourself and even scolded yourself for what you did? That's the indignation Paul is talking about.

A few weeks ago, I said something unkind to one of my daughters in front of her siblings. Immediately, in my mind, I tried to justify my comment. However, the Holy Spirit's voice was overpowering. I knew I had to apologize publicly in front of my family. I did. But I will tell you, I was so mad at myself for saying that to my daughter. This indignation has made me watch my tongue lest any stupid thing suddenly slips out again and causes injury to someone else's heart.

....

Confession brings a new enthusiasm to our lives to obey God.

....

Paul talks about fear being a virtue of confession. Fear in this context is a good thing. It is the distrust of our own ways. When we realize that our fleshly nature cannot be trusted, we are rightly afraid to give in to our desires. This fear causes us to "lean not on our own understanding" (Proverbs 3:5).

Our own desires and nature are not to be trusted. Our natural inclinations will get us into trouble. So when we begin to fear our natural inclinations, because of the trouble it got us into, we will distrust that nature and not be as apt to yield to it.

Acknowledgment of our sin produces a "vehement desire" to please God. When we understand the folly of our own desires and actions, we submit in greater measure to God. He sets a new course for our life. I liken this "vehement desire" to Romans 12:1, where Paul beseeches Christians to become living sacrifices to God. "Vehement desire" is when we begin to pray, "Have Your way in my life, Lord."

Zeal follows "vehement desire." Confession brings a new enthusiasm to our lives to obey God. We become passionate and joyous about following God's dictates and directives.

Finally, Paul spoke about the benefit of vindication. When we confess our sins, God becomes our defense. What could be better than having Him as our defense lawyer? Romans 8:33-34 puts it this way: "Who shall bring a charge against God's elect? It is God who justifies. Who is he who condemns? It is Christ who died, and furthermore is also risen, who is even at the right hand of God, who also makes intercession for us."

Jesus is our Lawyer pleading our case before God who is the great Judge. Jesus says to the Father, "They have confessed and I have forgiven." God then says, "Forgiven! Case closed!"

We Can Make the Right Choice

Satan will never stop lying. As long as we are living on earth, we will hear his lies and be tempted by them. We must remember that no matter what he promises, he is lying! His ultimate purpose is our death and the destruction of God's garden of purpose and beauty in your life. He will plant weeds of doubt about God's power. And he will celebrate each time we ignore God's direction and then blame everyone else for our decisions. When we do that, he is assured that we'll never deal with our disobedience and our avoidance of godly knowledge and truth.

Our strength to resist lies comes from knowing the triumphant work of Jesus on the cross. As we pray, stand on the promises of God's Word, and worship God we will grow more determined in our resistance and perseverance. Our desire, as women, to know the truth and to gain a deeper understanding of our hearts, needs, and our weaknesses will help us resist blaming the devil when we have the power of God to lean into.

It's time to refuse Satan and to stop giving him power by saying he has greater influence in your life than God does. Be ready to admit when you've blamed others for your wrong actions, words, and choices. Learn from your mistakes! Taking responsibility for your personal growth is your way of being prepared to resist the devil, to move forward in your unique purpose, and to walk in the garden trusting God and enjoying an intimate, honest relationship with Him.

As we explore the devil's encounter with Eve and go back to the garden to create a bouquet of wisdom, keep in mind that each path you take in your own garden relates to decisions you make. Even when circumstances have caused upheaval or heartache, your reaction to those circumstances and your willingness to trust God comes down to a choice. Will your heart surrender to Him? Will you let go of your wounds, your pride, your status, your anger and embrace His redemptive truths?

> *Dear Lord,*
>
> *I thank You for each one of the women reading this book. These precious women want to be set free from the lies that have held them captive. They want the freedom You offer. Will You help them, precious Savior, to recognize Satan in all the disguises he has worn and wears? Will You help them embrace the truth You are offering them?*
>
> *Let them see and embrace the beauty in the garden You have placed them in. Let them believe the truth of Your generous Spirit. Walk with them, talk with them, speak Your truth into their hearts and lives.*
>
> *Deliver them from deception and let them not be afraid to fully accept and walk in the truth.*
>
> *I ask these things in the powerful, invincible, and glorious name of Jesus, our Savior, Sovereign, and King!*
>
> *Amen!*

Questions for Study and Personal Reflection

1. Think about a time when you blamed someone else, your circumstances, the devil, or even God for your sinful actions or thoughts. What happened?

_____

_____

_____

_____

_____

2. What are your top three excuses for not reading God's Word? After you've written these down, re-read them. Are these the excuses you also give to avoid other acts of faith and obedience?

_____

_____

_____

_____

3. What desires have you struggled with? How has Satan played on your desires to lead you into temptation?

_____

_____

_____

_____

4. Read Luke 4:1-13.

   a. Comment on the way Jesus resisted each temptation.

_____

_____

_____

_____

_____

   b. What steps will you take against Satan's temptations?

_____

_____

_____

_____

   c. What have you learned about how Jesus resisted the devil?

_____

_____

_____

_____

5. Can you think of some quick fixes you have "accepted" in recent days, months, and years? Why did you accept them? And what motivates you to look for enduring answers now?

_____

_____

_____

_____

6. What excites you about taking responsibility for your spiritual growth? Make a list of the first three steps you want to take toward this life-changing goal.

_____

_____

_____

_____

Chapter 5

Lie: I'm Not Worthy

One day I was talking with my friend Kris, who has a vital counseling ministry, and I mentioned that after a recent conversation with a woman I knew, I felt totally inadequate. Kris practically leaped off the couch. "It's the 'less than' syndrome," she exclaimed. "There are people who will always make you feel 'less than' acceptable, 'less than' they are." Kris explained to me that many of the young men and women she worked with had been made to feel 'less than' by their peers or parents. These feelings of inadequacy made them seek out different means of escape.

As women we already have a propensity to feel "less than." After all, we are bombarded with the images of perfectly fit, precisely dressed, ageless, and beautiful women who boast about their perfect homes and successes. The curse of comparison is deadly, isn't it?

Perhaps you have been made to feel "less than" in one of the following areas:

less than a good Christian
less than a good decorator
less than a clean housewife
less than a good wife

less than a good mother

less than fit

less than thin

less than fashionable

less than intelligent

less than accepted by God

According to the Bible, we have been "accepted in the Beloved" (Ephesians 1:6). God has saved us because of His great love and not because of our goodness or our perfections. He does not give up on us because we are imperfect. In fact our admitted imperfections draw Him closer to us. He promised that His strength was made perfect in our weakness (2 Corinthians 12:9).

Almost every woman struggles with some sort of insecurity. One moment we are fine and the next moment all we can see are the faults and failings of our lives.

Finding Our Value

Tony always carried his Bible with him. He attended Bible studies at my church with regularity. Good-looking and confident, Tony seemed to be a born leader. There was a company of young men and women who looked to him for spiritual guidance and support.

He and I had talked infrequently at church and the conversations had always been upbeat with spiritual overtones. So when he asked me out, I was willing to see if this might be someone God had for me.

Tony showed up the next day at my house and announced that we were going to have a Bible study in Joshua together. I was elated. Joshua was one of my favorite books in the Bible. As a child, I had grown up with the adventures of Joshua. Not only did I have a background of ten years of Sunday school and Good News Club experience, I had also grown up under the discipleship and tutelage of my father, Pastor Chuck Smith.

Tony and I went outside and took a seat in the back garden. A gentle breeze fluttered the leaves of the trees that shaded us. He opened his Bible and I did the same. He started to speak with an introduction about who Joshua was. "Joshua was a slave in Egypt. He heard Moses' message to the children of Israel and became Moses' right-hand man."

"Yes!" I agreed enthusiastically. "He was from the tribe of Ephraim and no doubt—"

Tony cut me off at this point. Raising his hand to his mouth he said, "Uh-uh-uh…let the women keep silence."

I was incredulous. Tony was silencing me from sharing because I was a woman. To him, being a woman disqualified me from having anything of any worth to say about the Bible. That upset me!

"The Bible is full of women who spoke the Word of God. Miriam, Deborah, and Huldah were all prophetesses who were called to speak the Word of God to men," I countered. Again Tony raised his finger to his mouth.

"I sense that you do not have a submissive spirit," he said with an air of superiority.

Now I was getting angry. "You are not my husband, and nowhere in the Bible does it say that women are to be submitted to men in general. The Bible says—"

Tony interrupted my talking by raising his hand to his mouth a third time, again to silence me.

I stood up and looked down at him. I'm sure my face showed my shock and my frustration. Even though I was caught off guard, I was able to communicate what I wanted to, "I think you had better leave my house."

Now it was his turn to look incredulous.

I led the way from the back garden, through the kitchen, and out the front door without a word. I closed the door behind him. At that point I began to pray to my heavenly Father who loved me and called me His own.

My father had raised me with the assurance that Jesus loved me. I knew that I was equally important to God as my brothers were. My aunt had been a single missionary and served the Lord all her life. Missionary biographies of women who ministered in the name of Jesus had been my constant staples growing up. And I was well acquainted with the notable women of the Bible who were used by God. In fact it was Mary Magdalene who was the first person to see the risen Jesus. He told her to proclaim to the disciples the great news that He was alive. Imagine if Mary would've met Tony along the way! Right when she started to speak, he would have put his hand to his mouth and said, "Uh-uh—let the women keep silence!"

Those who consider women "less than" or always second to men have completely missed out on God's intention and love for women.

Feeling Less than Whole

Julie could barely speak above a whisper. And she was reluctant to meet my gaze. "I just always feel bad about myself."

It was difficult to ascertain how Julie could have any feelings of insecurity or condemnation. She had loving parents who were not only supportive but also concerned for her welfare. They constantly assured her of her talent and beauty but it fell on deaf ears.

You are of great value and importance to the God of the universe. It's time to believe that wholly.

During this time, Julie's tendencies to apologize bordered on obsessive-compulsive. She said "sorry" over and over again and took on a great sense of remorse and regret. The deception of unworthiness was becoming her distorted truth.

Julie reflected on the circumstances of her life. In her background was an abusive relationship that had failed. She pored over those circumstances with great deliberation, replaying scenes from that relationship in her mind and out loud in our conversations in her quest to uncover a fragment that would explain her present state. Every time she replayed her past, she felt more condemned and was plagued with more questions than answers.

I knew where Julie needed to go. And it wasn't to her past but to our beginnings in the garden. Together she and I explored the wisdom and insights we could gather from all that unfolded in Eden. She received the answers and the freedom she longed for. You and I will do the same. You are of great value and importance to the God of the universe. It's time to believe that wholly.

And God Made Woman

The first chapter of Genesis provides an overview of God's creation of the earth, the universe, atmosphere, the seas, sea life, plants, and animals. It was after the creation of all the animal kingdom on the sixth day of creation that God created the first man and woman. Genesis 1 concludes with their creation:

> *Then God said, "Let Us make man in Our image, according to Our likeness; let them have dominion over the fish of the sea, over the birds of the air, and over the cattle, over all the earth and over every creeping thing that creeps on the earth." So God created man in His own image; in the image of God, He created him; male and female He created them. Then God blessed them, and*

God said to them, "Be fruitful and multiply; fill the earth and subdue it; have dominion over the fish of the sea, over the birds of the air, and over every living thing that moves on the earth" (verses 26-28).

As God surveyed His vast creation of stars, moons, planets, atmosphere, seas, rivers, mountains, trees, plants, animals, and mankind, He saw that there was a deficit. And woman would be the one to fill that void. So God created the woman with artistry, beauty, and purpose. She was the great final touch in His creation. Only after He created Eve did God pronounce the whole of His workmanship as very good.

Each woman is "fearfully and wonderfully" made. Every woman is God's *poema*, or work of art (Ephesians 2:10). She is the culmination of His workmanship and without her, God could not and would not pronounce the whole of His creation good or bless what He had made.

You are God's workmanship. You have been created for divine purposes. He designed you just as you are to showcase His glory.

Does it surprise you, as it did my friend Julie, that the story of creation is more than a Sunday-school lesson to be heard as a girl and then forgotten as a woman? Julie was finally able to claim the truths, promises, and great love revealed in Genesis as a testament of her value in God's eyes. Once she claimed her identity as a special creation of a loving, caring God, she experienced the transformation that comes with believing the divine imprint is indeed on your heart.

After only a few weeks, Julie entered my office with a big smile and sparkling blue eyes that eagerly met mine during our conversation. Her relief and joy came from the freedom she found in that ancient garden.

Let Go of Insecurity—Embrace Your Identity in God

Scripture also states that both male and female were created in the image of God. That means that women also have a divine aspect to their lives. His image is stamped on our frame and design as well as on the design and frame of men. You might correctly make the declaration that you are a Designer piece!

I think it is this divine aspect that makes every woman want to be a princess. It is not by accident that little girls are drawn to Cinderella, Sleeping Beauty, and Snow White. These princesses, I believe, represent something latent in every woman and that is the relationship they were created to have to their Creator. The King of kings designed women and stamped His own signature in their unique and grand framework.

My mother was well aware of this divine aspect to her framework. She had never known her real mother or father. She was placed in the care of an older couple at seven weeks of age and then legally adopted by the same couple when she was 14. One day I asked her why she didn't try to discover her true heritage. With a sweet smile and a sparkle in her blue eyes she looked at me. "Well, I always wanted to believe that I was really a lost princess. I am not ready for that ideal to be laid to rest." For an inquiring young woman that was the perfect answer. I could possibly be the grand-daughter of royalty. My mother could be an unclaimed princess hidden in the shadows of common humanity. This wonderful ideal inspired many imaginative narratives in my fertile imagination.

My mother keenly felt that divine image that was inscribed upon her creation. One of her favorite psalms was Psalm 45. She loved where it read,

> *Listen, O daughter,*
> *Consider and incline your ear;*
> *Forget your own people also, and your father's house;*

So the King will greatly desire your beauty;
Because He is your Lord, worship Him.
And the daughter of Tyre will come with a gift;
The rich among the people will seek your favor.

The royal daughter is all glorious within the palace;
Her clothing is woven with gold.
She shall be brought to the King in robes of many colors;
The virgins, her companions who follow her, shall be brought
*   to You.*
With gladness and rejoicing they shall be brought;
They shall enter the King's palace (Psalm 45:10-15).

The royal image was stamped upon every woman through our ancestor Eve. Every woman bears a bit of that residual glory stamped on her image. That image of divinity is what God promises to revive through Christ Jesus and bring us back to the royal position that He originally intended for women. That is why each woman has the secret desire to be a princess within her heart.

Created for Glory

You matter to God. As we walk through the different lies that many of us need to release our hold of or be released *from* we will discover that many of these lies could have been sidestepped had we claimed this important truth: You matter to God. And from the very beginning, women were created for His glory—for beauty, love, and great purpose.

When we look at Genesis, we realize the great attention God gives to His creation of man and woman. You might be surprised to discover that Adam's creation has an honorable mention, but there is an entire chapter to describe why and how God created woman. I'm not saying that makes us more valued or valuable than men. However, this focus in Genesis helps us understand why we are here and why our role and purpose is of great importance to God.

We find that after God created light, He "saw the light, that it was good" (Genesis 1:4). After God created the seas, He "saw that it was good" (verse 10). After God created the fruit-bearing trees, "It was good" (verse 12). When God made the lights to shine in the universe He "saw that it was good" (verse 18). God also saw that the creation of animals was good (verse 25). However, in Genesis 2:18, God sees something that is "not good." That thing is man's loneliness. God says, "It is not good that man should be alone." Something essential was missing. You got it—that missing piece to complete the perfect picture was woman.

God could not bless His creation in its incomplete state. He recognized that His creation was lacking, so He created woman to fill the deficit that was needed. After creating woman He blessed His creation and pronounced it "very good."

You Are Blessed

When God proposed to remedy the deficit in creation He stated that He would make a helper for man that would be comparable to him. This phrase, "helper comparable to him" includes the Hebrew word *ezer*. This word is also used in Psalm 33:20 in reference to God being our help. So rather than a position that is lower than man, God's intention for woman is to be someone to aid or help man. Woman was created because man without her was deficient. Man, like the rest of creation, needed help and completion. This completion was supplied by God in woman.

Man also needed companionship. He needed someone who

was like him, but different. Man needed someone who would complement his life and bring fullness to his person.

But before God created woman, He allowed Adam to feel his deficit. He presented all the animals before Adam. Adam named all the animals. Among the entire animal kingdom there was not one creature that could serve as a fit companion for him. It was necessary that Adam see his lack. Often that is just what God does. He allows us to see our deficit before He supplies the answer or the need. In this way He grasps our attention and appreciation for the gifts He is about to give. So with Adam God showed him his need of companionship and the insufficiency of the rest of creation to fulfill that need before He presented Eve to him.

God caused a deep sleep to fall on Adam. As Adam slept He removed part of the side of Adam's body. From that portion of skin and tissues, God fashioned Eve. Many Bibles read that God took a rib from Adam to create woman, but the Hebrew word is actually *tsela*. This word is used 41 times in the Bible and is only translated as rib in Genesis 2. The other 39 times it is used it refers to the side or the corner of an object such as a building. There is a Hebrew word for rib and that word is *khomesh*. But that is not the word used here. God took a part of man, not just a rib, but also man's flesh and man's bone to create the first woman.

Years ago I heard a brilliant Christian scientist say that Eve was the first clone. Her tissues were made from Adam's bone where the cells are produced. Eve was not created from lesser materials than Adam but from the same materials, because God intended Eve to be Adam's companion, his equal, but with her own unique qualities. It is a powerful realization when you understand the glory of your workmanship and your worth to God.

After creating Eve, God brought her to Adam. God presented His workmanship, and what a workmanship she must have been, because Adam looked at her and announced, "This is now bone of my bones and flesh of my flesh; She shall be called Woman because she was taken out of man" (verse 23).

God blessed all of His creation. That means men and women. "Then God saw everything that He had made, and indeed it was very good." Woman was created by God and in His image...and she was blessed.

God Esteems Women

The Bible is filled with the stories of women who were used extraordinarily by God. These women were not standouts because of family lineage or other forms of status. They were important and used by God because they made their lives available for His purposes. They were willing to do whatever He asked of them in their various walks of life.

Sarah, Abraham's wife, became the matriarch of Israel. What did Sarah do to achieve such prominence? She believed God's promise to her husband and went on an extended camping trip throughout the land of Canaan. If you don't think that is significant, try camping in the woods for two weeks. Then you will appreciate Sarah's contribution. She lived in tents with Abraham for over 50 years. She lived in a land she was unfamiliar with. She lived separated from her relatives by vast deserts.

In Canaan, at 90 years old, Sarah gave birth to Isaac. Isaac would be a patriarch of Israel (Genesis 17, 21).

Rebekah, who would marry Isaac, went from insignificant to significant when she agreed to return with Abraham's servant to Canaan to marry Isaac. Before that time, Rebekah was a virgin living with her family in Mesopotamia.

When Rebekah heard the testimony of Abraham's servant, she wanted to be in the plan of God. Though her family urged her to delay, she chose instead to go back to Canaan as soon as possible.

Through her obedience to God's call, Rebekah also became a matriarch of Israel (Genesis 24).

....

God not only uses women in His purposes, but He raises
them from insignificance to significance.

....

Deborah was a mother in Israel. She was the wife of a man named Lapidoth. She came to prominence as a judge and prophetess. She would communicate to the Israelites both the Word of God and His directives. He used Deborah's obedience to His Word to deliver the nation of Israel from the oppression of the armies of Sisera (Judges 4–5).

Abigail is another of the many outstanding women mentioned in the Bible. She lived with a cruel and selfish husband named Nabal. One day, David, who would later become the king of Israel, sent a request to her husband, asking to come with his men to Nabal's celebration. Nabal rudely refused the request. When Abigail was told about her husband's rude behavior, she prepared food for David and his men and traveled with it to where he was staying.

Abigail not only appeased David's anger, by her actions, she saved Nabal's household. Later after his death, Abigail became the wife of David.

All this came to Abigail because she believed God's promise concerning David, that he would one day be the king of Israel. She did what was necessary to aid him and his men. In so doing, Abigail encouraged, nourished, and blessed David (1 Samuel 25).

God not only uses women in His purposes, but He raises them from insignificance to significance. These women were all raised from obscurity simply by believing, applying, and obeying God's Word.

Jesus Loves You

In the Gospels we find Jesus giving special attention to women. One of His first miracles was healing Peter's mother-in-law (Matthew 8:14-15). Another time He moved through pressing crowds to raise a little girl to life again. As He was being thronged by the crowds, He paused to minister to a woman who had suffered for 12 years from a physical ailment. He drew attention to her and showed her great respect as He addressed her as "daughter," a term of great respect and dignity (Matthew 9:18-25).

When Jesus visited Tyre, the only person He tended to (who is mentioned in Scripture) was a Canaanite woman whose daughter was demon-possessed. He not only delivered the woman's daughter from a demon but publicly commended her faith (Matthew 15:21-28). He often visited the house of Mary and Martha, and John records that "Jesus loved Martha and her sister" (Luke 10:38-42; John 11:5). During the course of His ministry, Jesus insisted on going to Samaria. He sat by a well and waited for a Samaritan woman to come that He might reveal to her the way of salvation. After His resurrection Jesus commissioned Mary Magdalene to deliver the news of His resurrection to His disciples.

Woman's original estate was unique, beautiful, full of purpose, and glorified. That original intention of God has been marred but not diminished. It is possible to return to His original intentions for purpose and glory through a relationship with Jesus Christ. As we look at Jesus, God incarnate, we see Him esteeming, loving, and elevating women to a respectful estate. He desires to reinstate the glory of womanhood to you.

You bear the stamp of God, but that divine stamp can only be realized as you submit your life fully to the purposes of Jesus. You are worthy, my friend. You are worthy of the life God has planned for you. Take that to heart and let it sink in and affect all that you are and all that you do.

Questions for Study and Personal Reflection

1. When have you felt less than whole?

   _____

   _____

   _____

   _____

2. Has someone or some event in your life made you feel unworthy of love and purpose?

   _____

   _____

   _____

3. Read about the creation of Eve in Genesis 2:18-25. What does this say to you personally about your value?

   _____

   _____

   _____

4. Imagine yourself as a genuine Designer piece. What feelings rise up when you consider the stamp of royalty that is on your heart and soul?

   _____

   _____

   _____

5. How do you want to live out your sense of value as the King's daughter? What changes do you want to make? How will you make these changes?

_____

_____

_____

_____

6. Thank the Lord for awareness of your worth. Feel the strength and beauty of being an individual made in God's image and saved by the blood of Christ. How will you live out life as a blessed woman of God today?

_____

_____

_____

_____

Chapter 6

Lie: The Grass Is Greener Everywhere Else

Eve had a wonderful life in the garden. She walked among the trees, flowers, and animals and enjoyed fellowship with Adam and God. She lacked for nothing. All that was needed for a whole and good life was provided courtesy of a loving, attentive God.

But that all changed after her dialog with the devil. Satan made Eve feel like she was lacking something.

Though Satan never actually told Eve she was lacking something, it was the impression he gave her. That is often how he operates. It is not always what the devil says outright, but the impression that we are left with. It is the impression that something is wrong with what we do have or how we are. And we start to look around to see what we might be missing. That's when the dissatisfaction takes root and begins to spread from your mind to your heart. Soon your attitude and actions reflect a growing desire to look for what is lacking in your life. It becomes easy to disregard all that you do have and all that you are when your sights are set on that which you shouldn't have, can't have, or don't have.

Dissatisfaction plagues so many women today. It hits you without warning after you run into an old friend who seems to have her life so together. It fills your thoughts after watching a romantic movie or reading a novel. It can follow the discovery of new lines on your face. When the restlessness of discontentment stirs within you, you will have difficulty viewing your circumstances through the lens of truth.

When you feel those first stirrings or maybe when you recognize that those stirrings have become influential directives in your life, it is vital to let go of them. If you allow them to build, they will distort your view of self, God, and others. They will make you thirst for things that are not of Him, and then when you achieve the goal of those ungodly pursuits, you will not be satisfied.

You and I will explore how dissatisfaction distorts our perspective so that we can understand our truest longings…the ones God has placed within us, His beloved daughters.

The Destructiveness of Dissatisfaction

Joanne sat across from me on the couch. Her arms were crossed tightly against her chest. Outwardly she had everything a woman could desire. She had a large house, a new car, a perfect figure, three beautiful children, and a husband who adored her.

She pressed her body against the back of the sofa, trying to put as much distance between the two of us as possible. It was obvious she didn't want to be alone in the room with me. Her husband had arranged our meeting. He had tried to draw her out with no success. He hoped that she could explain to me the reason for her attitude and actions.

As much as I tried to probe in order to draw her out, Joanne answered every question with a nervous laugh and the phrase, "I just don't care." She feigned indifference but it was obvious that resentment and anger rested just behind the façade.

She was determined to venture out into this wild, unknown territory no matter the cost to her family, her self-worth, or her spiritual health.

Lately, according to Joanne, she had simply grown tired of her life. She longed for excitement, something different. She had become fixated on the Internet's opportunities to meet and converse with strange men. She had even covertly met one of these men and become infatuated with him, until she found out that his background was less than admirable. However, rather than dampening her interest, this had incited it. She actively sought out men, even dangerous ones to correspond with.

She knew her husband was heartbroken. She knew her older daughters were disgusted. Yet her continued response was to laugh lightly and shrug. When I asked her where the dissatisfaction with her life came from, she didn't give it much thought before responding, "I've been over all this in my mind a thousand times, and I've decided I just don't care. I don't care where this desire for something else came from. It's here and I feel I must act on it."

No dissuasion on my part seemed to faze her. She was determined to venture out into this wild, unknown territory no matter the cost to her family, her self-worth, or her spiritual health.

"You remind me of another woman I read about," I remarked casually.

Joanne raised her eyebrows in mock curiosity. I continued. "Like you, this woman had a beautiful place to live and a loving husband. Like you she became dissatisfied with her life after conversing with someone she unexpectedly met."

She looked interested now. She leaned forward. "What happened to her?"

"Well, she acted on her dissatisfaction and did what she knew was wrong. And she lost everything. She lost fellowship with God. She made a decision that could never be reversed. She lost her ageless beauty and she gained a life that would involve shame and remorse."

"Yeah? Well, at least she tried," Joanne retorted. "I have to try."

"I don't think she ever believed it was worth the gamble." I tried one last appeal. "Joanne, do you ever pray?"

"I do pray. I often ask God to forgive me for what I am doing and for what I am going to do."

"I don't think that prayer works. God listens to the prayer 'Not my will but Yours be done.' There's a great life out there, Joanne, but you won't find it where you are looking."

Again the nervous laugh and the final, "I don't care."

I warned her as strongly as I could about the road she was on. She remained as indifferent as when she had entered my office. With great sadness, I watched her walk away and toward a series of the same mistakes.

Unfortunately, Joanne's sense of dissatisfaction is not unique. It seems like every other day I hear about or talk to women who are dissatisfied with their lives. It doesn't matter how much they are loved or how much square footage their home takes up, dissatisfaction plagues their minds relentlessly. Few of them can cite the source of their dissatisfaction. And many of them, like Joanne, reach a place of indifference when they've lived in a state of disconnection from God and His purpose for too long.

Longing for What You Don't Have

Satan had persuaded Eve to turn her attention away from all

she had and to focus only on what she was not allowed to have. Her perspective was obscured. Because of her hyperfocus on the forbidden, she lost sight of all the blessings in her life.

That's how it had been for Carolyn. I met Carolyn at a retreat in the mountains of California. I was leading a time of open sharing before communion. During this time, many of the women stood to testify how the Lord had spoken to them or ministered to them during the retreat.

I had noticed Carolyn earlier. She kept to herself during the retreat and when she did speak, she was very guarded. She was a beautiful middle-aged woman. Her dark hair was styled perfectly and her clothes were classy and refined. But while her physical appearance was inviting, her demeanor was as blatantly distancing as a "Do not disturb" sign.

When she stood up to share her story, tears were pouring down her face. She spoke in a soft, Southern accent. "Women, I married my college sweetheart who I met at church. He was the kindest man I had ever known. Together we purchased a great big house and started raising a family together. My husband worked hard to spoil me.

"After we had been married for ten years, I met a handsome younger man at our church. He was dashing and said all of the right things. He started being very attentive to me. I was flattered at first and then infatuated.

"I soon forgot about my husband, my house, and my children. We started an affair, and I was sure that I had found the love of my life and my soul mate. Nothing would satisfy me but to live the rest of my life with this new man.

"My husband was crushed when I told him of my decision to leave him and start a new life with my beau. My children were angry, but I was enthralled. I left my family and together we moved to Southern California. When my divorce was final, we married. We were together for two years when he left me for another woman.

"Here I am now. My first husband wants nothing to do with me. My children won't speak to me. I am estranged from all of them. I have no home. I work full-time and I am so bitter. Oh sisters, pray for me and the bitterness in my heart."

Carolyn scanned the audience of women who sat stunned and attentive, and then she continued with a plea, "Take inventory of all God has given you. Be thankful for your husbands that work so hard. Hug and love your kids. Don't let anyone draw you away from all you have. Don't end up like me, a bitter woman."

When she sat down, everyone was quiet. I closed the time of sharing with prayer and proceeded to the communion service. Carolyn raised her hand. No one had ever before raised his or her hand during communion. I looked at her and her face looked ashen. "I think I am having a heart attack," she said.

Two nurses rushed toward her. I sent a friend to call the paramedics while I directed the rest of the women out of the auditorium and upstairs to a different meeting room for communion.

Carolyn was rushed to the hospital where it was confirmed that she'd had a heart attack. The doctors said that though she was only in her forties, her heart was weak. She was sure her bitterness was the cause of the attack.

I will never forget Carolyn or her admonition to all of us women: "Take inventory of all God has given you." If only Eve had taken inventory of all God had given her.

Too easily we lose sight of all that God has given us. When we lose sight of all His blessings in our life, we are vulnerable to the lies of the enemy.

Be Careful What You Wish For

Satan suggested to Eve that the means to personal enhancement was through disobedience to God. "For God knows that in the day you eat of it your eyes will be opened" (Genesis 3:5). Well, we can all attest to the fact that Eve's eyes were certainly opened after she took that bite. She was aware of sin, shame, guilt, and what it felt like to be separated from God's will. Not exactly the power and perspective she had hoped for.

The lie that God's way is limited, confining, and restricting has become prevalent in our modern society. It's no wonder that we are tempted to open our eyes and to look for something better than what we have. When we start glancing around and become certain that the grass on the other side of the fence of obedience and faith is much greener and more attractive, then we have already started to peer out at the world with a tainted vision rather than to look for God and seek His desires with our hearts.

What influences you and distorts your view of how green the grass is on the other side? There are songs, movies, magazine articles, and novels proclaiming freedom and satisfaction through sin. These polished, pretty offerings are much of what Satan wants to pitch to us as the "better life." There are women experimenting with all sorts of destructive behaviors in the hope of finding fulfillment.

Sin definitely opens your eyes, but not to beauty. It opens your eyes, heart, and life to shame and regret. Many women have been duped into losing their priceless dignity and security by some of the influences I listed.

Alice learned this lesson the hard way. She had loved growing up in her Christian home. She hadn't minded the restrictions her parents had placed on her. They seemed reasonable and beneficial: no sex before marriage, no drugs, and a reasonable curfew.

However, she fell in with a bad crowd in high school. At first she felt strong enough to accompany her new friends without engaging in their practices. After a time, the pressure mounted, but she continued to resist the temptation.

However, it wasn't long before Alice's view of her parents' restrictions changed. Her take on these reasonable precautions became distorted. By exposing herself to temptation over and over, she was allowing her strength and conviction to be worn down. Now the rules made to protect her seemed too binding and ridiculously rigid.

Alice didn't like the emotions which surfaced when she was in this new world of ungodly behavior. Instead of feeling proud and protective of her innocence, she became embarrassed by her ignorance about drugs and alcohol. Her friends seemed so sophisticated and informed. They soon convinced her that her parents were keeping her from all the fun things in life. "After all," they reasoned, "your dad said that before he was a Christian he did drugs. You need to experience life like he did."

She began by smoking pot with her friends. By the time she was 18, she had graduated to narcotics. One day, desperate for help, she confessed everything to her parents. Immediately they got her the help she needed.

Alice's eyes were now fully open. She knew every drug and its nickname. She knew what life on the streets was like. She knew what it was to be hung over. She knew the degradation of addiction. What she hadn't found in the forbidden was freedom or fulfillment.

Let Go of Discontentment—Embrace Fulfillment

Moses was confronted with the same choice as Eve. He, like Eve, was offered a seemingly easy way out of his immediate situation.

However, he chose to "suffer affliction with the people of God" instead. That doesn't sound like a smart trade-off by the world's standards, does it? But if we examine the story, we'll understand that Moses was making the remarkable decision to pursue the fulfillment of God's purpose for him over all else. And great things would happen as a result:

> By faith Moses...refused to be known as the son of Pharaoh's daughter. He chose to be mistreated along with the people of God rather than to enjoy the fleeting pleasures of sin. He regarded disgrace for the sake of Christ as of greater value than the treasures of Egypt, because he was looking ahead to his reward. By faith he left Egypt, not fearing the king's anger; he persevered because he saw him who is invisible. By faith he kept the Passover and the application of blood, so that the destroyer of the firstborn would not touch the firstborn of Israel.
>
> By faith the people passed through the Red Sea as on dry land; but when the Egyptians tried to do so, they were drowned (Hebrews 11:24-29 NIV).

What an interesting selection he made! The Bible tells us that he made this choice because he recognized that there was no fulfillment in sin—in following a way that was against God's will. He had a chance at the easy life or simple solution, but it would've been the long way around to a life of his purpose. And if he hadn't been true to God's calling on his life, we'd be reading very different stories about the Israelites.

Moses chose authentic fulfillment through obedience to God. Even though his decision would entail hardship and difficulty, he was sure of the choice. He didn't want a temporary fix that would leave him wanting. He said "pass" to the temptation of letting himself off the hook because he wanted the true fulfillment that comes by serving God.

Saying "Pass" to the One-Bite Promises

Too many women go for the temporary fix. I call these false promises "The One-Bite Solutions." Consider the following promises:

- eternal youth in a face cream
- perfect contentment in a relationship
- happiness in a drug
- perspective in a movie
- fitness in a machine
- renewed health in a surgery
- serenity in a drink
- confidence in a new outfit
- instant wealth in an investment
- sophistication in a cigarette
- help in a bottle
- vigor in a vitamin
- security in a home
- peace in a philosophy
- utopia through a political leader
- wisdom in a book
- peace in a new location

Every one of these false hopes leaves you disappointed and still thirsty. Think back to our other review of quick fixes. Do you see how easily the temporary bit of comfort or relief can become our preference? Convenience will never offer the fulfillment of everlasting truth and revelation. If your eyes are now opened to how silly these promises seem in the light of personal revelation and God's purpose, let's look more closely at what truly fills us as women of God.

The Well That Never Runs Dry

God offers us a means to never be thirsty, hungry, or in want of anything. Does that sound too good to be true? The Samaritan woman thought the same, but as she spoke to Jesus by the well, she soon became convinced that she was indeed speaking with the all-knowing Messiah. And what He offered her was so much more than she could have ever dreamed of that day at the well.

This portion of Scripture is very exciting and revealing about the nature of Jesus. He is so forthcoming and kind in His exchanges with the woman. Read the following selection from the book of John. Imagine what it would be like to be having this conversation with the Lord right now:

> *He [Jesus] was alone at the time because his disciples had gone into the village to buy some food.*
>
> *The woman was surprised, for Jews refuse to have anything to do with Samaritans. She said to Jesus, "You are a Jew, and I am a Samaritan woman. Why are you asking me for a drink?"*
>
> *Jesus replied, "If you only knew the gift God has for you and who you are speaking to, you would ask me, and I would give you living water."*
>
> *"But sir, you don't have a rope or a bucket," she said, "and this well is very deep. Where would you get this living water? And besides, do you think you're greater than our ancestor Jacob, who gave us this well? How can you offer better water than he and his sons and his animals enjoyed?"*

Jesus replied, "Anyone who drinks this water will soon become thirsty again. But those who drink the water I give will never be thirsty again. It becomes a fresh, bubbling spring within them, giving them eternal life."

"Please, sir," the woman said, "give me this water! Then I'll never be thirsty again, and I won't have to come here to get water."

"Go and get your husband," Jesus told her.

"I don't have a husband," the woman replied.

Jesus said, "You're right! You don't have a husband—for you have had five husbands, and you aren't even married to the man you're living with now. You certainly spoke the truth!"

"Sir," the woman said, "you must be a prophet. So tell me, why is it that you Jews insist that Jerusalem is the only place of worship, while we Samaritans claim it is here at Mount Gerizim, where our ancestors worshiped?"

Jesus replied, "Believe me, dear woman, the time is coming when it will no longer matter whether you worship the Father on this mountain or in Jerusalem. You Samaritans know very little about the one you worship, while we Jews know all about him, for salvation comes through the Jews. But the time is coming—indeed it's here now—when true worshipers will worship the Father in spirit and in truth. The Father is looking for those who will worship him that way. For God is Spirit, so those who worship him must worship in spirit and in truth."

The woman said, "I know the Messiah is coming—the one who is called Christ. When he comes, he will explain everything to us."

Then Jesus told her, "I AM the Messiah!" (John 4:8-26 NLT).

Are you going to the well that never runs dry to meet your needs and to satisfy your longings? Think about how it must have felt to be this woman at the well. She held onto much shame and sin. Her physical needs brought her to the physical well. But as soon as Jesus spoke of living water, her heart recognized the deeper spiritual need. She needed a Savior. She was thirsty for forgiveness and the eternal refreshment of salvation.

> Be a woman who worships the Father in spirit and in truth and you will never be in want.

My dear sister in Christ, you and I are that woman at the well. God knows our every sin, weakness, desire, and hope and He loves us unconditionally. He might quench the immediate need you have in your life because He is a giving Lord. But there is so much more to receive from your Savior. The bucket will not be empty. When you return to the well for satisfaction and renewal, you will never be denied. The Lord will be there to provide life everlasting.

"But the time is coming—indeed it's here now—when true worshipers will worship the Father in spirit and in truth." There's that beautiful, refreshing word: "truth." Be a woman who worships the Father in spirit and in truth and you will never be in want.

As Jesus told the woman at the well, "'Anyone who drinks this water will soon become thirsty again. But those who drink the water I give will never be thirsty again'" (John 4:13-14 NLT). Our worldly vision of what will fill us, satisfy us, and give us a richer, better life is so, so limited compared to what God offers us. It's great news that we are designed to be filled with the living water.

God has placed us in His garden and supplied us with His water of life. Is Satan offering you a greener garden, a different spring, something outside of God's will? Stop! It's a lie. Look around at all God has given to you. Drink from the water He has given you. Don't lose all you have because of a lie.

Questions for Study and Personal Reflection

1. How has dissatisfaction crept into your mind and heart? Write down any specific times you recall when you allowed it to enter your life.

_____

_____

_____

_____

2. When have you pursued the "greener grass" and felt the sting of realization that your troubles follow you? What lies were you holding onto instead of the truths of the Lord?

_____

_____

_____

_____

3. Describe a time when you didn't take the easy way or the way of temptation and you stood grounded in God's best for you. How did it feel during and after the point of decision? How can this experience nurture your strength today?

_____

_____

_____

_____

4. How does revisiting the story of Moses inspire you to view
   God's path for your life with a deep sense of satisfaction and joy?

_____

_____

_____

_____

5. What spiritual need brings you to the well of the living water?

_____

_____

_____

6. Describe your thirst for contentment. What do you long for?
   Take those longings to Jesus in prayer today. Write out your
   prayer or journal about it. Jesus is ready to meet you at the well.

_____

_____

_____

_____

7. List ten beautiful things in your life. Write a short note of gratitude for each one.

1. _____

_____

_____

_____

2. _____

_____

_____

_____

3. _____

_____

_____

_____

4. _____

_____

_____

_____

5. _____

_____

_____

6. _____

_____

_____

_____

7. _____

_____

_____

_____

8. _____

_____

_____

_____

9. _____

_____

_____

_____

10. _____

_____

_____

_____

Chapter 7

Lie: God Doesn't Speak into My Life

When Brian and I were first married, we were both learning the new roles we had accepted as husband and wife. Neither one of us were settling easily into those roles. While on a trip, we had a fight that kept us from speaking to each other for two hours.

Stuck on a plane and unable to communicate with each other because of our pride, we both tried to occupy ourselves by reading our Bibles. I glanced over at Brian's text and noticed he was reading Ephesians 5. I knew that Scripture contained a word to husbands about loving their wives. I was ecstatic. I knew an apology would come soon. Brian kept staring at the open Bible. He didn't turn the page. He sat there deliberating over the passage. I could almost feel him wrestling with the Holy Spirit.

Then I glanced down at my passage while I waited for the apology. *Oh no!* I thought as I saw 1 Corinthians 13, the chapter on love, waiting for my attention. That day, as we let go of our pride, the Word of God worked in both of us to forgive and show grace and love to each other as God intended. That was over 31 years ago!

God's Word equips us with all we need to live godly lives. It supplies us with right doctrine or teachings about God, salvation, sin, and prophecy. It sets us straight when we start to get off track. It instructs and teaches us how to please God. Paul highlights the divine quality of the Bible: "All Scripture is given by inspiration of God, and is profitable for doctrine, for reproof, for correction, for instruction in righteousness, that the man of God may be complete, thoroughly equipped for every good work" (2 Timothy 3:16-17). Our faith journey, identity, and relationship with Him are made complete through the power of His words working in and through our lives.

The Supernatural Work of God's Words

A Christian woman I know claimed she never heard the voice of the Lord. Another woman in her Bible study group challenged her to keep a journal next to her when she read her Bible. "After you read a selection of Scripture," the woman instructed, "write down everything you learned as you read."

The woman complied. She began to fill her journal with inspirational words the Lord gave her as she read. She realized then that He had been speaking to her, but she hadn't taken the time to listen. Now that she recognized His voice she was able to hear Him speak.

The Bible shows us the way things need to be done. Psalm 119:105 promises that God's Word will be a lamp to our feet and a light to our path. When you spend time in Scripture and in prayer to listen for His voice, you will experience a light lit from within too. You will be changed supernaturally. Psalm 19 speaks of some of the divine ways that His Word works in us. According to verse 7, His Word converts our soul. To *convert* is to change the nature of something. I love this possibility.

A Whole New Perspective

When I was a young girl, I loved it when my father got a convertible. On a rainy day, our car had a roof that kept us from getting wet, but on sunny days, the roof came down and we had the delightful experience of driving through town and by the beach with a complete view of the beauty that surrounded us. It was a perspective that often went unnoticed during the colder seasons. I noticed the sky, the birds, the clouds, the brilliant warmth of the sun. It was an entirely different journey. In much the same way, the Word has the capacity to change our very nature and our journey. It changes our hearts and our experience through the roadways of life.

The Bible does more than just give us knowledge, directives, and information. It fills us with wisdom. When we immerse ourselves in Scripture—pray it, trust it, and live our lives by its truths—the limits of sin-clouded perspective are lifted.

During one plane trip, I sat next to a woman who was from upstate New York. She explained that her job was to train teachers on how to instruct children to write. She shared about her methods and the successful results teachers had in the classroom when they were implemented. I was very impressed. A bit later she asked me why I was traveling. I explained that I was teaching from the Bible at a women's retreat. She then asked me if she could get my advice on some issues she was struggling with.

She explained the difficulties of her present circumstances. For each of her difficulties, I gave her a corresponding scripture or biblical example. After I shared, she smiled. "You are one of the wisest women I have ever met. Where do you get your wisdom?"

I was able to share with the woman the source of my wisdom— the Word of God. I encouraged her to read the Bible. Enthusiastically she promised me she would.

The Bible equipped me to help this woman.

When I moved back from England, I struggled with depression for over a year. I cried out to God for relief. Then one day at the women's Christmas coffee at our church, the speaker recited Jeremiah 15:16: "Your words were found, and I ate them, and Your word was to me the joy and rejoicing of my heart; for I am called by Your name, O LORD God of hosts." It was the answer I was praying for. I had been reading my Bible but not ingesting it. I hadn't been taking it to heart. I had been reading the Word out of discipline and duty but not mixing it with faith and thanksgiving. I went home and dove into my Bible, thanking God for every promise. My joy returned that day.

......

We might not recognize the devil immediately, but we can recognize the aftereffects of listening to him.

......

God's Word also enlightens our eyes (Psalm 19:8). The Bible will give us hope and creativity. When we read about the victories of those who followed the Lord and leaned on His directives, we are filled with hope for our own battles.

The stories of biblical characters like Abraham, Jacob, Joseph, Jonathan, and David offer encouragement, instruction, and insight for the challenges we face. The Word of God literally brightens our perspectives and fills us with hope for what He will do.

Psalm 19 further states that God's Word warns His servants. He desires to keep us from harm. His Word warns us of impending danger, the devil's devices, and foolish behavior. The Bible warns us by way of cautions, commandments, stories, and examples. The aftereffect of God's Word is hope, joy, security, and assurance.

Have you ever had a conversation that drew your attention to the forbidden? Perhaps the conversation made you turn inward, or made you feel like you were lacking. Satan presents his coercive comments and suggestions in different ways. Like Eve, we might not recognize the devil immediately, but we can recognize the aftereffects of listening to him.

When your focus is drawn to the God-given prohibitions in your life, or to your own fulfillment, or to your inadequacies, realize that you are listening to the wrong voice! Get back to the Bible!

God's Word Speaks into Our Lives

God's Word speaks divine strength, encouragement, love, and grace into our lives. The more we read and meditate on the stories, encounters, testimonies, and instructions of the Bible, the more we grow in spiritual attributes. Second Corinthians 3:18 speaks of this transforming work. "We all, with unveiled face, beholding as in a mirror the glory of the Lord, are being transformed into the same image from glory to glory, just as by the Spirit of the Lord." There is a cooperative work going on as we meditate on the Word of God. As we meditate the Spirit of God is free to divinely work the life and attributes of Jesus into our heart and mind.

When the Word of God Does Not Work

To me one of the most tragic passages of Scripture is found in Luke 5:17-26. In this passage several men bring their paralytic friend to see Jesus. Undeterred by the crowds, the young men hoist their friend up onto the roof. They tear off the tiles and lower their friend on his pallet right down into the midst of the crowd gathered in the house to hear Jesus.

Jesus, perceiving the faith of the young men, pronounces the paralyzed man forgiven. The Pharisees immediately take exception to Jesus' assertion that He has the power to forgive sins. He reiterates His power saying, "That you may know that the Son of

Man has power on earth to forgive sins…I say to you, arise, take up your bed and walk."

The paralytic is immediately healed. He stands up and walks right out of the midst of the crowd, carrying the pallet that once carried him.

So what is tragic about that story, you ask? Luke reports that "the power of the Lord was present to heal them" (Luke 5:17). It is tragic that only one man was healed. I am sure there were many in that crowd who needed healing. However, because they refused to believe that the Son of God had power on earth to forgive sins, they were left in the condition in which they came.

Though these men heard, saw, and were in the presence of Jesus, their unbelief kept them from the divine touch of God.

In the same way, if we refuse to believe in the power of God, we will not be healed in whatever way God plans to heal us or work through our trial. The author of Hebrews says that the children of Israel could not enter the promises of God because of unbelief (Hebrews 3:19). The author then warns his readers that we also can come short of a promise of God if we do not believe. "The gospel was preached to us as well as to them; but the word which they heard did not profit them, not being mixed with faith in those who heard it" (Hebrews 4:2).

To experience the power of God's Word we must believe it.

God's Word Is for You

Kayley was a young woman in the throes of critical decisions. She was overwhelmed. After praying she checked her e-mail. She noticed a note from an older woman that she was well acquainted with but hadn't heard from for quite a while. The woman wrote that she felt prompted by the Lord that morning to write to Kayley to tell her that the Lord had good plans for her future. At the end of the inspiring note the woman had put the Scripture reference Jeremiah 29:11.

Kayley quickly looked up the scripture. She read it out loud taking each word to heart. It was the very word she needed and she felt a sense of kinship to the verse. "I know the thoughts that I think toward you, says the LORD, thoughts of peace and not of evil, to give you a future and a hope."

Peace welled up in Kayley's heart. This peace was followed by an assurance that God was with her and would guide her future toward peace and happiness.

That afternoon, as she was shopping, she walked into a gift store. Her eyes were suddenly drawn to a plaque on the wall that was for sale. In bold green letters on a beige background it read, "I know the thoughts that I think toward you, says the LORD, thoughts of peace and not of evil, to give you a future and a hope." She felt a surge of joy and excitement. The Lord was with her.

When she got home she opened her mailbox and gathered the letters that were inside. She noticed a card that looked interesting. Tearing open the envelope was a short note from her aunt in Northern California. On the front of the card was Jeremiah 29:11. Kayley almost laughed out loud. She looked toward the sky and prayed, "Thanks!"

She began to notice the verse everywhere. She saw it on mugs, T-shirts, and book covers. Each time she read it she felt as if she was getting a personal reminder from God. This verse was her verse.

About two weeks later, Kayley was at a home Bible study. After the teaching had ended, the host invited everyone present to share something the Lord had been speaking to them lately. Kayley couldn't wait to tell her story. However, before it was her turn another young girl spoke up.

"The most amazing thing happened to me last week! I was asking the Lord for direction when I noticed a small business card on the ground. Picking up the card I read Jeremiah 29:11, 'I know the thoughts that I think toward you, says the LORD, thoughts of peace and not of evil, to give you a future and a hope.'" The girl went on to elaborate the different and exciting ways that God spoke Jeremiah 29:11 to her.

Kayley's heart sank as she heard this testimony. That was her verse, or was it? Had God really been telling her that He had her future under control? She thought back to the e-mail, the plaque, and the note. Perhaps she had been reading too much into it. The girl's story sounded much more divinely inspired than her own testimony.

I talked to Kayley a week later. She poured out her whole story to me. "Do you think God meant that verse for me?"

"Yes," I answered emphatically. "He meant it for you and for her, and He delivered it to both of you with His own personal touch!"

Have you ever felt like the Lord was speaking to you through a specific Bible story or scripture only to have someone else claim that as their personal revelation from God? I've had this experience. At the time, like Kayley, I was ready to believe that God hadn't really spoken to me until a wise woman told me that He speaks His promises to all His children.

Believing the Wrong Voice

When we feel cut off from God's love, we can fall into temptation more easily. Have you ever believed the voice of Satan over the voice of God? Or have you looked back on a situation in your life and realized that you paid attention to Satan's lies instead of God's truths? Paying attention to where our thoughts originate from is vital. Satan fills us with a sense of condemnation. He'll cause us to believe that we are distanced from God or unloved by Him. The sudden thought that Jesus doesn't love us will hit us out of nowhere. That's how it was for my oldest son when he was just a boy.

It seemed like Char would be plagued every night just before he fell asleep by some condemning notion. One night he was sure that God didn't want him in heaven. Another night he was afraid that God didn't hear him when he prayed. Each night Brian and I would sit with him, explaining spiritual realities to him, and then pray with him.

As soon as one battle abated another ensued. This time Char felt condemned over the bad thoughts that he had. Again, we explained the origin of those thoughts and listened as he prayed his boyish heart out to Jesus.

Brian told Char the story of C.H. Spurgeon, who had gone through a similar experience when he was a young man. He too had been plagued by bad thoughts. Spurgeon confessed these thoughts to his grandfather. His grandfather turned kindly eyes on him and asked, "Do you enjoy these thoughts?" Spurgeon answered that he hated and despised them.

The wise grandfather responded, "Then don't claim them. They don't belong to you. They are from the devil."

At a young age Char learned to bring every thought into the captivity of Jesus Christ as instructed by Paul in 2 Corinthians 10:5.

This is a great practice for any believer. Take every thought captive and surrender them to the Lord. In this way, Satan's thoughts and suggestions are defeated. It is not a one-time action but needs to be a continual practice. Every day we are bombarded by demonic suggestions. We must take each thought, as often as they come, and simply give them to Jesus.

When a persistent thought attacks my mind, I choose a specific person to pray for. Every time that thought is suggested I start praying for that particular person. I've decided that when Satan attacks I will fight back by claiming territory for Jesus.

I suggested this practice to a young woman who couldn't seem to get the victory over her thought life. She chose to pray for a little boy who had leukemia. One day she commented to me that she was sure he would be healed because of how often she was praying for him. She must have prayed a lot because that boy is a young man now and perfectly healthy!

When Satan Speaks

You can recognize Satan by the subject matter he wants to talk about, the doubts he suggests, and the aftereffects of the conversation. And the more you know the voice of God, the more you'll be able to distinguish between the speaker of truth and the speaker of lies.

Eve had been perfectly content in the garden of the Lord. She lived among the uncorrupted beauty of God's trees, flowers, and plants. She ate the finest of fruits from any tree she desired except the tree of the knowledge of good and evil. She was able to wander about with a menagerie of tame animals from lions to cuddly bears. Adam was her faithful and perfect companion. (Think about that! What woman hasn't dreamed about the perfect man?)

She was able to renew herself from the refreshing springs that flowed out from the garden to form four burgeoning rivers.

And Eve knew the voice of God.

Yet, as she heard the deception and the doubt that filled the serpent's conversation, she did not compare that to the truth, power, and goodness of God's voice and message.

Eve had felt no sense of want, discontentment, or failure *until* she began to talk with the devil.

Dangerous Dialog

The handsome flight attendant bent down to address me. "So I got a report that the plane is being flooded by the tears of two women."

My friend and I laughed. "That might be accurate," I confessed. "I really admire C.S. Lewis and I was really touched by the movie you just showed about his marriage to his wife, Joy."

The attendant glanced briefly at the front of the plane where a screen had been displaying the movie and asked, "You like C.S. Lewis?"

"Yes. I have read quite a few of his books and I love the way he talks about God and about His Son, Jesus."

The attendant's face visibly soured. "Oh, so are you a Christian?"

"Yes!" I answered enthusiastically. "I believe that Jesus is the only Son of God and that He came to earth to identify with the plight of men, and then to die for our sins. I also believe that He rose from the dead and is at the right hand of God right now."

I could see that the conversation was not going well. I paused a moment to pray and ask the Lord to speak through me.

For a short time he feigned interest in the conversation. "So would you like to meet up sometime and tell me more about Jesus?"

"Well, I would love for you to meet my husband. He could tell you more about Jesus."

The sour look returned. "I don't want to meet your husband. I want to meet with you. Why don't you give me your phone number and we can make arrangements?"

"No. That isn't a good idea. My husband is a great guy with a dynamic understanding of God's Word. I think you'd really like him. If you give me your number, I'll have him call you."

"Can't you meet with me? Is your husband the jealous type? Don't you have freedom?"

I could see that the conversation was not going well. I paused a moment to pray and ask the Lord to speak through me. As I did this, I noticed a woman who was knitting across the aisle. She held up her hands in a praying position and winked at me before going back to her knitting. (This was before the time when knitting needles were considered lethal weapons on airplanes.)

Sensing my apprehension, he grew a bit more aggressive. "I hate women like you who think they are so righteous that they can just go to heaven."

"Oh, I'm not going because I am so good—I am going because Jesus is so good and His blood is so powerful that it has forgiven and cleansed me of every bad thing I have ever done. That same forgiveness and cleansing can be yours and you can have absolute certainty that you are going to heaven."

"I need to attend to the other passengers right now, but I have something I want you to read."

He walked down the aisle to the back of the plane. I turned to my companion who had been praying for me. "There's something not right here," I whispered.

"No. You are doing great," she responded.

Still, my uneasiness persisted.

He returned a short time later and thrust a book in my hand.

"Read this," he said while pointing to a paragraph. "That's written by a Christian."

He turned on his heel and left me with the book. I started to read. The paragraph was borderline obscene. It contained heavy sexual content.

Coming back up the aisle he wore a seductive smile. "What did you think?"

"I think a book like this should be saved for a married couple."

"I bet your marriage is not as happy as you think. If you had a secure marriage you would be willing to give me your phone number."

As kindly as I could, I told him that because my marriage was secure and because my husband was one of God's greatest blessings in my life, besides my four children, I was not willing to give him my phone number or meet with him. I told him there were many churches he could go to and meet someone there if he was sincere. In the meantime, I volunteered to pray for him.

The conversation was over!

Disembarking from the plane, I still felt the sting of some of the barbs. However, waiting at the gate was my beloved husband. He looked like a gift from heaven.

Have you ever had a conversation that is so dark that it left you feeling insecure and questioning things you always knew to be true? Perhaps, unbeknownst to you, you were dialoging with the devil.

Uncertainties about our actual beliefs can rise up for many reasons during a deceptive conversation. If you've had a long season of grief or struggle, you might wonder if God has forgotten about you. You might question if God has decided to cut you off from communication. Don't let this be your belief, my friend. You know His voice and He will not quit speaking to you. Allow there to be times of stillness and prayer and patient waiting. It is difficult, but the exchange of lies for truth is worth it.

Let Go of Confusion—Embrace Clarity

Jesus promised in John 10:27 that His sheep hear His voice and another voice they will not follow (John 10:5). It is vital that you learn the sound of your Shepherd's voice.

All of my life people have called me on the phone and pretended to be my dad by imitating his voice. I have never once been fooled. I not only know the sound of my dad's voice, but I know the subject matter he likes to talk about and the phrasing he uses when he talks to me. Others don't know these secrets. My father has been talking to me all my life. My mother sat through many sermons while she carried me in her womb and she said that I was born knowing my father's voice. It is a familiar voice to me because I have heard it for so long.

In the same manner, the Lord's voice will become familiar to us the more we hear it. The best way to know the voice of Jesus is to read the Gospels again and again. Personally, I think everyone should read a portion of the Gospels each day. As you read them you will become accustomed to the way in which Jesus speaks. The more you know His voice, the more readily you will recognize the voice of the devil.

As Jesus said, "Another they will not follow."

Knowing God's Voice

My father used to always say the devil badgers and condemns while Jesus invites and convicts. There is a big difference between being pressured and being drawn. The devil uses bullying methods to intimidate us. He makes us feel that we need to give an immediate response or reaction.

Jesus draws us by His loving-kindness. He invites us to come and follow Him. There is no badgering but a constant gentle invitation to follow Him.

Satan condemns us and makes us feel like there is no hope for us. The condemnation leaves us with no way out.

Jesus convicts us by letting us feel the shame of our sins yet at the same time offering forgiveness for them. He promises a restoration of fellowship if we will simply confess our sins. The Bible says that if we confess our sins, God will be faithful and just to forgive us our sins (1 John 1:9).

People have often asked me how I can discern the Lord's voice. I have learned to recognize His voice by the nature of what He talks about and the certainty of the impression I feel when He speaks. Unlike my emotions that often shout at me, His voice has a calming effect. It always coincides with the Scriptures. He never contradicts His written Word.

The Lord's voice is always pointing me in the direction of the promises and commandments of the Bible.

There is really only one sure way to acquire an ear for the voice of the Lord and that is to daily read the Bible. The more you read His Word the more you will learn to recognize His voice when He speaks to you.

Steve had been saved only a few months when he called me on the phone and related an impression he had. As he was waiting for the carpet cleaner to arrive at his apartment, he sensed the Lord telling him to witness to the carpet cleaner. Steve called to ask me if I thought it might really be the Lord. I said I thought it very well could be. We prayed together before he hung up.

Two hours later, Steve called back. Sure enough, after he shook hands with the carpet cleaner a conversation ensued. Steve shared his testimony with the carpet cleaner, and the man prayed with him to accept Jesus into his heart.

This is often how believers hear the voice of the Lord.

Jesus Whispers

Years ago, when we lived in England and my youngest son was a little boy, he had a very naughty day. Usually Braden was well-behaved, but that particular day, in the midst of company and an inspection by our landlord, he had chosen to show his worst side.

It began with Braden walking on the roof of the car and refusing to climb down when one of my friends told him to. His response was a defiant, "You're not my mom!" Later the landlord scolded him for scaling an ancient wall that was in need of repair. This reprimand was also met with the response, "You're not my mom!"

Later that afternoon I noticed a sticky substance on the walls of our living area. While our guests congregated in the kitchen, Brian and I interrogated each one of our children. When we came to Braden he reluctantly confessed he had thrown an apple core against the walls of the room. When asked why he replied, "Because I wanted to."

As we were wiping the apple core from the walls, I noticed there were gaping holes in my wicker chairs. I asked Braden if he knew who was responsible for the damage. He shrugged his shoulders as if he didn't care. Then with a careless demeanor acknowledged breaking off bits of the wicker to provide weapons for his army men.

He was disciplined and sent to our room to meditate on his actions. We would have sent him to his own room, but we had guests sleeping in every spare place.

After Brian and I had dealt with Braden, we entered the kitchen to comfort our guests, who were feeling a bit sorry for him. The weather outside was frigid but everyone in the kitchen was dripping with beads of sweat. "It's awfully warm in here," my friend Rose commented.

Noticing the warmth myself, I went to check the thermostat.

Sure enough, someone had turned it to 40 degrees Celsius or about 104 degrees Fahrenheit. Immediately I knew who was responsible!

Brian and I found him crying in the room. "Braden, did you turn up the thermostat?"

After he admitted he had, I sat down on the bed. "Braden, you have had a very naughty day and done a lot of things that were naughty." Hiding his face in the pillow, he shook his head in agreement.

"Braden," I continued. "While you were doing those naughty things, did you ever hear Jesus telling you not to do those things?"

Braden removed the pillow and gave a wailing, "Maybe."

"What do you mean maybe?" I asked somewhat frustrated.

"Well the devil keeps yelling and Jesus just whispers!" he loudly lamented.

Brian and I had to turn away so Braden couldn't see the amused look on our faces.

It is funny to me how Braden, in the midst of his naughtiness, got it right. Satan's voice is demanding and condemning. There is always harshness to his tone. However, Jesus' voice will always be kind and compelling.

The Fruit of Listening

Your faith in God's Word will be evident through your obedience to it. Obedience is the activity of faith. When we obey it, we will find that God will divinely work in us. You will experience the abundant fruit of listening to your Creator.

....

Satan will try to lie to you and tell you that God's Word
only works in other people's lives but has no
power in yours. Don't believe him.

....

Satan does not want God's divine work accomplished in us for a number of reasons. The first reason is that Satan desires our destruction because he hates God's creation. Secondly, he knows that if God works divinely in us we will be a light and draw others to Jesus. Thirdly, as Jesus divinely works in us through the power of His Word, we become a threat to the kingdom of darkness as we claim the promises of God for our life.

Satan lied to Eve when he told her that she would not die. He directly contradicted the power of God's Word. He will try to lie to you and tell you that God's Word only works in other people's lives but has no power in yours. Don't believe him.

The word of God is living and powerful, and sharper than any two-edged sword, piercing even to the division of soul and spirit, and of joints and marrow, and is a discerner of the thoughts and intents of the heart (Hebrews 4:12).

The power that spoke the universe into existence and continues to sustain it is the same power that works in your life as you read and believe His Word and the words He speaks into your life.

Questions for Study and Personal Reflection

1. Read Psalm 19 and highlight the qualities of God's Word. Which ones stand out to you right now?

_____

_____

_____

_____

2. What work do you desire God's Word to work in your life?

_____

_____

_____

_____

3. When do you feel the most alone? What can you do during these times for comfort?

_____

_____

_____

_____

4. Read John 10:29 and list some of the characteristics of Jesus' voice.

_____

_____

_____

_____

5. For this week, choose a portion of Scripture that you will read and re-read each day. Take time to make notes after each reading. What is God's Word teaching you? How does revisiting the same verses allow you to go deeper and hear His voice in a new way?

_____

_____

_____

_____

_____

Chapter 8

Lie: I Can't Be Forgiven

She looked scared. When I saw her inching her way forward down the church aisle, the phrase "a deer caught in the head-lights" immediately came to mind. Tina was a short, stout, and mature woman with unruly red hair. Surrounding her was a bevy of women from her home church. They had brought her to the retreat, and they were the ones pushing her forward.

"How are you doing?" I asked in my friendliest tone, trying to assuage her fears.

She answered back in crisp, cold sentences. "I am fine. And I don't need this." She was not only scared—she was annoyed. The women circled around her and joined hands. The woman closest to her spoke endearingly, "See, we all love you. Most of all Jesus loves you. You have nothing to be afraid of." Tina stiffened at these sentiments. It was obvious that she didn't believe them.

Earlier Tina's pastor's wife had approached me. "I brought a woman named Tina with me to this retreat. She is feeling so con-demned and she said she is ready to bolt out of here." I found this a strange reaction to the messages I was giving.

The theme of the retreat was taken from Matthew 11:28-30:

*Come to Me, all you who are weary and are heavy laden, and
I will give you rest. Take My yoke upon you and learn from Me,
for I am gentle and lowly in heart, and you will find rest for your
souls. For My yoke is easy and My burden is light.*

During each session I had stressed the grace of the Lord. I talked about the gentleness and love of Jesus. I shared that He desires us to come just as we are with all our faults and failings. How was it possible that after hearing about the love and abounding grace of Jesus, Tina felt so condemned?

Each woman in the circle took turns saying an encouraging word to Tina. I watched this embarrassed grandma shrink under the added attention. She looked down and shook her head from side to side. She was trying hard to hold back the tears that were waiting to pour out.

Finally, I traded places with the woman beside her. "Tina, I want to stand next to you. I know how you feel." She looked up at me. This time a wave of hope seemed to cross her face. I threw my arms around her and simply hugged her tightly. The other women burst into prayer.

"What is it, Tina? What's holding you back?" I whispered into her ear.

Under her breath, she began to answer, "I shouldn't be here. You don't know how bad I've been. There's no forgiveness for me."

"There is, Tina. The blood of Jesus is greater than anything you could have done or will ever do," I said soothingly. Then I told her again that I knew exactly how she felt.

Resisting Grace

When I was a freshman in college I gained a great deal of weight. I didn't want any of the other girls to know how desperately I missed my mother and father, so to cover the pain and anxiety, I ate. I remember one time eating a huge bowl of peanut butter, jam, and corn chips all mixed together. Yuck!

The more I ate, the more condemned I felt. One day my room-mate offered me a solution. Her mother had given her some herbal laxatives. She told me that every time she overate she simply took some laxatives and passed her entire meal right through her digestive system. It sounded like a quick and wonderful fix. The next time I overate, I simply swallowed two of the herbal pills.

Well, the next thing I experienced was a stomach wrenching in torment. My whole body trembled. Waves of nausea poured over me. In the midst of this grueling pain I heard a voice whisper to me, "You deserve this pain, you glutton!" In my weakened state, I believed the voice. I accepted the pain as the just recompense for my overeating.

A vicious cycle ensued. Condemned over my overeating, I would take the laxatives and endure the pain. After a painful ordeal, sometimes lasting all night long, I would resolve to diet. My diets always included some strenuous exercise routines and little nourishment. I felt these regimens were necessary for a girl who could not control her appetite.

Due to the intensity and unrealistic measures of my various resolutions, I would fail rather quickly. After each failure, I mollified myself with overindulgence in some sort of food. You can guess the pattern. After each episode of indulgence, I used the herbal laxatives. So the cycle continued throughout my freshman year of college.

The lie that I couldn't be forgiven was
tormenting me emotionally, physically,
and spiritually.

I tried everything to break it. I wrote in my journal. I prayed. I talked to my resident assistant in my dorm, but she was also in the cycle. I cried. I went on diet after diet. I resolved. I promised. I withdrew. I found every scripture in the Bible I could find that pertained to overeating and wrote them out and pinned them up on the walls of my dorm room. (I really only found two in Proverbs and they were taken out of context, but I thought any scripture on gluttony would do me good.) I mentally chastised myself.

In this time of what felt like constant failure, I struggled to allow forgiveness to cover me. I felt paralyzed by this hidden shame. I became a recluse. During church and Bible studies my heart and mind were restless. When I would hear about the promises of God, I felt disqualified to receive them. I desperately wanted to be a part of all the benefits and blessings that were in Christ, but felt unfit to claim them.

Meanwhile, I struggled with jealousy. Girls around me ate whatever they wanted with no restraints and no condemnation. They didn't struggle with binging or purging. Everyone in the world looked beautiful, happy, and carefree. I resented them for it.

The lie that I couldn't be forgiven was tormenting me emotionally, physically, and spiritually.

I have talked with, prayed with, and counseled many women who have struggled with this same lie.

Topsy-Turvy Theology

We seem to believe that our sin, whatever it is, is bigger than God's grace. Somehow our theology is turned upside down when we have done something wrong. We are disoriented and in our time of uncertainty, we question His power to overcome our sin. Though the issues vary, the deception remains the same:

I can't be forgiven because I overeat.

I can't be forgiven because I overspend.

I can't be forgiven because I keep failing.

I can't be forgiven because I was unfaithful to my marriage vows.

I can't be forgiven because I killed a child growing in my womb.

I can't be forgiven because I lied.

I can't be forgiven because I betrayed a friend.

I can't be forgiven because I keep losing my temper.

I can't be forgiven because I've hurt the people I love.

I can't be forgiven because I can't forgive myself for what I have done.

I imagine this is just how Eve felt in the garden. It was she who listened to Satan. It was she who chose to disobey God's command. It was she who picked the fruit from the tree. It was she who took the first bite of the forbidden. It was she who convinced Adam to eat the fruit. Eve must have felt that she was the cause of every ill that befell her and Adam. Perhaps at one point she even felt that she deserved every iota of her punishment.

Destructive Detours

The nature of this lie leads to many destructive paths. One of those roads is the one that leads straight to self-defeat: *I will never be good enough so I might as well stop trying.*

Another danger of this type of mentality is self-sabotage. We can become our own worst enemy. Our thoughts begin to echo the cruel taunts of Satan. Whatever name he calls us, we call ourselves.

We might even cause ourselves physical harm because we believe we must be in charge of our own destruction. I wonder how often Satan gets to take the day off because we are so ready to take over the demise of our sense of value and belief that God loves us.

Today there is a disturbing, destructive practice among girls, including Christian girls, of cutting themselves with razor blades because they are so hurt, sad, broken, or filled with shame. They are cut off from their emotions and it actually becomes a comfort to them to feel *something*, even if it is physical pain. It becomes either their controlled form of punishment or their release. They are so hungry for relief and so unbelieving that they deserve grace.

Talking to one of these girls, I asked what led her to do something so desperate. She told me it was her inability to be perfect. Every mistake she made was punished with a cruel cut of the blade against her skin. She wasn't satisfied until she saw the oozing of her blood. Then she would say to herself, *There! You deserve that! If you don't want another cut then don't blow it again.* This might seem to be extreme, but think about how God feels when we cut down ourselves with yet another sharp-edged put-down or we decide that we aren't worth saving, so why return to His open arms?

Trying to Earn Forgiveness

When you believe you can't be forgiven, you might find yourself looking for ways to *earn* the forgiveness of God. This mode of striving to be worth His grace can become destructive, because it is in Christ that you are worthy. There is nothing that you do that makes yourself achieve a certain, passable level of value. That's why it is grace. And if you keep trying to earn or replace His grace with your own actions and power, you'll experience frustration, anger, and resignation. These are symptoms of this lie.

The lie "I can't be forgiven" is one of the most devastating lies that Satan whispers to women. It is effective because at the core of our being we feel the guilt and shame of our actions. He mixes every lie with a grain of truth.

When the devil sought to tempt Jesus, he used portions of Scripture, saying, "It is written…" Within every one of those temptations was a morsel of truth from the Scriptures.

The truth is, we *do* fail. The truth is, we *have* sinned. The truth is we do deserve punishment for our sin. The truth is, we have done terrible things. The Bible clearly states that "all have sinned and fall short of the glory of God" (Romans 3:23). The Bible also declares that "the wages of sin is death" (Romans 6:23). The payment for the sins we have committed is death. That is the morsel of truth that is mixed in with the lie.

The lie screams that our sins are greater than the forgiveness offered to us through the sacrifice of Jesus Christ. The lie takes the morsel of truth that deals with the reality and due penalty of our sin, and denies the power and efficiency of the blood of Christ to pay for our sins. At the same time the lie refuses to acknowledge the greatness of God's love and desire to forgive men and women their offenses. Yet it was God who sent His only beloved Son into the world "that whoever believes in Him should not perish but have everlasting life" (John 3:16). A right understanding of the true nature of God coupled with a belief in the power of Jesus' cleansing blood will set us free from all lies.

The greater truth that defeats the lies is found in the rest of Romans 6:23: "The wages of sin is death, but the gift of God is eternal life in Christ Jesus our Lord." The Bible also states, "There is therefore now no condemnation to those who are in Christ Jesus" (Romans 8:1). In John 8:32, Jesus said, "And you shall know the truth, and the truth shall make you free." It's in knowing, realizing, and walking in the greater truth that we are set free from the condemnation and torment of the lie that says God cannot or will not forgive our sins. When we immerse ourselves in His vast forgiveness, we are able to forgive ourselves.

God desires to forgive our sins. He wants to answer our prayers. He wants to restore our fellowship. He wants us to know the glory of the abundant life He has promised. Unconfessed sin will keep us from that glory.

Refusing to Admit You Were Wrong

I have often wondered what would have happened if Adam and Eve had simply said, "We were wrong." You and I have looked at how vital it is to uncover the lies we believe and the lies we use to protect ourselves from losing pride, taking full responsibility for our faith journey, and voicing our sins. We should find, once again, that Genesis offers us such a wealth of wisdom. We see again what *not* to do when we have faltered. Do not hide. Do not refuse to be vulnerable before the Lord. And do not take the easy out of placing blame elsewhere.

What are the three hardest words in the English language to say? Could they be "I was wrong"? Why do those words seem to stick in our throat? I think the word "sorry" is much easier to say. It can slip off the tongue with very little sincerity attached. "Sorry" can even be said with a rebellious attitude. It can even be used to make the other person regret calling us on our folly. However, that is not how it is with the phrase "I was wrong." It's difficult to say that insincerely.

> You can bring your time of weakness
> to the Lord with complete belief that He
> will listen to you and will cover you
> with His amazing grace.

To admit to a mistake or a weakness is tough because we don't want to be identified as the woman who was wrong last Tuesday (or any day of the week for that matter). It is easier to hide among the trees, as Adam and Eve did, than to admit wrongdoing. As we've explored throughout this book, it seems easier to embrace a lie than to stand in the spotlight of truth.

Years ago I was playing Monopoly with my kids. The two oldest were in a tight competition with each other, when my eldest daughter handed all her properties, hotels, and railroads to her little brother. That made the six-year-old an instant winner against his big brother. At the news that he won the game, Braden jumped up and did a tremendous karate kick in the air.

The problem with his victory kick is that it hit me square in the right eye and knocked me over. I could feel my eye swelling immediately. I got some ice and went to lie down on my bed. A few minutes later I heard Braden sniffling outside my bedroom door.

His older sister, sure he was feeling bad for kicking Mom, knelt down to talk to him. "Are you okay, Braden?" I could hear her ask outside my door.

"No," he answered tearfully.

"What's the matter?" she asked comfortingly.

"Well, everyone feels sorry for Mom and they don't realize that her eye made my foot hurt."

I would've laughed out loud if my eye hadn't hurt so badly.

No matter what the age, it's hard to say "I was wrong." Even if it has been 15 years since your transgression, you can confess your sin. You can bring your time of weakness to the Lord with complete belief that He will listen to you and will cover you with His amazing grace.

Confession

Confession is what God desires. First John 1:9 promises that if we confess our sins, He is faithful and just to forgive us our sins and cleanse us from all iniquity. Confession is admitting what we have done wrong.

There are two different elements involved in confession. It is not only an acknowledgment of what we have done, but also, it is the realization that what we have done is wrong.

I know when my children were young and acted badly, what I wanted more than anything was an acknowledgment of what they did and why it was bad. I wanted to make sure that they understood why it was wrong. If they acknowledged their bad behavior, I felt that the issue was resolved. If they refused to acknowledge their bad behavior, they were sent to their room to think about the behavior until they understood why it was wrong.

My mother used to warn me, "If you come to me directly when you have done wrong, then I will go easier on you. However, if I hear it from someone else or find out another way, you will be in big trouble." I gave that same advice to my children.

Confession is healthy for the soul and the spirit. We have all heard the saying "Get it off your chest." It can also be good for the body. Confession has been found to lower blood pressure, boost the immune system, and take a burden off the mind.

David spoke about the oppressive burden of unconfessed sin in Psalm 32:3-5.

> When I kept silent, my bones grew old through my groaning all the day long. For day and night Your hand was heavy upon me; my vitality was turned into the drought of summer. I acknowledged my sin to You, and my iniquity I have not hidden. I said, "I will confess my transgressions to the LORD," and You forgave the iniquity of my sin.

If you are struggling with confession, I invite you revisit our earlier, more in-depth exploration in the chapter "Lie: The Devil Made Me Do It." Our culture is not keen on confession, but it is a crucial part of the Christian life and of your path of forgiveness.

Grace Has More Power than Sin

Too often women view God's capacity to forgive as contingent upon the severity of their sin or the number of times they have tried and failed. They impose a limit on God's grace. Have you ever thought, *That had to be the limit. God can't possibly forgive me again?* When we think, say, or believe this, we are actually displaying more faith in the power of our sin and failure than in the power of the blood of Jesus.

God's grace is greater than the greatest and most heinous sin. God's grace is more extensive than the multitude of every failure of every person combined.

To grasp this grace—you must simply believe it. You have to simply reckon it to be so.

Grace by its very nature cannot be earned. It is a gift. There is no work or labor that you can do that will make you worthy of the grace of God.

Some people misguidedly believe that if they do enough good works they will be deserving of His grace. By thinking in these terms they belittle its greatness. God's grace is unreachable apart from faith. He, knowing there was no way that man could ever attain it, made it accessible through faith in Jesus.

When men asked Jesus what they could do to do the work of God, He answered, "This is the work of God, that you believe in Him whom He sent" (John 6:29).

Believing is the only way to receiving.

Let Go of Guilt—Embrace the Grace

Not everyone feels forgiven. Those who wait to believe they are forgiven until they feel it, rarely receive the full benefit of it. They have the cart before the horse. Faith precedes feeling. The grace of God must first be believed apart from feeling.

When we don't embrace the grace we are missing out on the greatest adventure. Jesus promised life and that more abundantly in John 10:10. He was talking about a quality of life that would bring fulfillment and joy. There are many promises waiting to be claimed by believers who will simply embrace the grace. The apostle Paul, in Ephesians 1:3, after greeting the believers in the grace of God, speaks of the multitude of blessings waiting for us in heavenly places in Christ Jesus. Psalm 31:19 also speaks of these blessings when it states, "Oh, how great is Your goodness, which You have laid up for those who fear You, which You have prepared for those who trust in You in the presence of the sons of men!" These blessings are meant to benefit us now, in this lifetime! The gateway to the abundant life is through the entrance way of grace.

It doesn't matter how great the sin or how many times the offense was committed. God's grace is greater. He is calling you into fellowship with Him and He has made that possible through Jesus Christ. Just accept it. When you are tempted to doubt it, just repeat, "There is power and wonder in the precious blood of the Lamb!"

Believing in Grace

What is this grace that must be believed? Grace, in its simplest form, is the free gift of God. It begins with His greatest gift, the forgiveness of our sins through the effectual blood of Jesus Christ.

God, in His infinite grace, desired a relationship with mankind. He created Adam and Eve that He might have fellowship with them and walk with them in His bountiful garden. Satan entered that garden and drew Eve away from the gifts of God by offering different gifts. Eve, tantalized by his offerings, disobeyed God and forfeited the right to God's goodness.

The consequence of her sin, and Adam's too, was that they were expelled from the original intimacy they had with God and the intended blessings of the garden. The benefits that once flowed freely were withdrawn, and Adam and Eve were made to toil in frustration.

God longed to fellowship again with mankind but sin stood in the way. His righteous nature was lethal to sin. No one who sinned could see God and live. Consequently, since every man and woman after Adam and Eve sinned, no one could see God.

Satan took advantage of God's invisibility to spread all sorts of vicious rumors and lies about Him. Though God spoke through the prophets of the Old Testament and had them write down His words, His character was still maligned, misconstrued, and misunderstood.

God continued to reach out to men. He chose Abraham to be His spokesperson and promised him He would raise up a nation of descendants. God made a covenant with Abraham's descendants. He wanted these children of Abraham to communicate His goodness and desire for a relationship with the world. However, the descendants of Abraham fell victims to the lies of Satan. Though God continually reached out to them, blessed them, delivered them, and spoke to them through the prophets, they turned their back on Him. They worshipped images and idols rather than the living God. In turn, He was forced to separate Himself from His people.

Yet He did not give up. He had a greater plan. He chose to send His only begotten Son, Jesus, to the people He had chosen. He announced the coming of His Son through the prophets a thousand years before He would come. God gave many signs through the prophets so that the descendants of Abraham would recognize their Messiah.

As foretold, Jesus came to the earth. From the time of His birth, He pleased God. He lived an absolutely sinless life. He resisted every lie of the devil and lived in total surrender to God. He showcased the character and personality of God. Men had misunderstood God so He brought God's goodness to the light. Jesus loved men and women. He healed all those who came to Him in need. He opened the eyes of the blind. He reached out to everyone in need. He told people about the true nature of His Father.

Then Jesus allowed wicked men to arrest Him, beat Him, mock Him, scourge Him, slander Him, assail Him, and crucify Him like a common criminal. Yet, God was working in the crucifixion of Jesus to reconcile the world to Himself.

The sinless blood of Jesus shed on the cross was the very element that was needed so God could forgive men their trespasses and sins. Jesus offered up His life on behalf of all men so that through His life men might be reconciled to God. Second Corinthians 5:21 states that God "made Him who knew no sin to be sin for us, that we might become the righteousness of God in Him."

Jesus shared His Father's desire to bring men and women back into fellowship with God. In John 17:24, Jesus prayed that God would use His death to allow men to enter into that fellowship:

> *Father, I desire that they also whom You gave Me may be with Me where I am, that they may behold My glory which You have given Me; for You loved Me before the foundation of the world.*

Jesus died on the cross as the ultimate sacrifice for sin. Then after three days in the grave, He rose again for our justification.

His resurrection proved the effectual power of His death. His resurrection is the assurance that our sins are forgiven through believing in Him.

Forgiveness is the first and greatest benefit of grace. Faith in the work of Jesus is the only entrance into the grace of God. Though there are many aspects and benefits to His grace they cannot be realized until one believes and receives by grace the forgiveness of their sins by Jesus.

It's only by believing in His grace and giving ourselves over to it that it becomes our experience, our hope, and our inspiration.

When Grace Is Experienced

The only way I was set free from the vicious cycle of bulimia was by believing that Jesus loved me even when I overate. He loved me even when I failed to live up to the high standards I set for myself. I had to choose to believe that He wanted to wrap His arms around me even though I thought I deserved to be distanced from God for overeating and for giving myself over to hollow attempts to solve my own problems.

I had to allow Jesus to love me even when I felt totally unlovable. I sang songs to myself about His love. I played music at high levels in my car about His love. I hungered to have the incredible truths of God's unconditional love and grace resonating throughout my every cell.

At the same time I was struggling with the lie that I couldn't be forgiven, God gave me a living example of His forgiveness.

On a Saturday morning, I drove with three other students down the highway to an amusement park about two hours away from our college. Anxious to get there and not paying attention to what I was doing, I suddenly saw a flash of blue and red lights in my rearview mirror. I pulled the car to the side of the road. The officer informed me how fast I had been traveling. I didn't really know how fast it had been until he told me.

I fumbled trying to find my driver's license and the registration for the car. Honestly, the officer who gave me the ticket was very kind to me. Of course I cried and felt so disappointed in myself.

School ended before the notice to appear in court arrived at my parents' home. By this time I had already informed them about the speeding ticket.

Mom, Dad, and I were scheduled to leave on a trip to Hawaii the day after my court appearance. Dad volunteered to drive me back up to Ventura to pay the fine. As we drove up there he made no mention of the ticket. There was no condemnation. Instead he talked about all the things we would do when we got to Hawaii.

Entering the courthouse I found out that I would have to appear before a judge. I was terrified. Dad sat right next to me in the courtroom as we both waited for my name to be called.

When my name was called I stood and approached the bench. The judge took the opportunity to tell me in every way possible what a loser I was. He threatened me by saying that if he ever saw me in his courtroom again he would make me do jail time. He was visibly angered at the speeding teenager he saw before him. I felt like dirt.

....

God has paid the penalty for the sins we are guilty of
committing so that we might enter the adventure
He has for us. He wants our fellowship.

....

I felt the full weight of my guilt. I was ashamed. By speeding, I had carelessly broken the law. I deserved every word he said.

The judge dismissed me after assessing the amount of the fine.

When I returned to my seat, my dad handed me the check. While the judge was reprimanding me, Dad had been filling out the check to pay the debt I owed.

Dad escorted me to the desk where I submitted the check. Once we were out of earshot he turned to me and said, "Now let's go to Hawaii!"

It was incredible. I began to weep. "You mean you forgive me? I am totally guilty and I have no excuse for what I did. I'm so sorry."

Dad put his arm around me. "I know that, angel. It's over now. We paid the fine and we can go to Hawaii."

"No, you paid the fine. I owe you."

Dad smiled one of those wide grins that only he could and said, "I'm your father and I love you. I want you with me in Hawaii. You don't owe me anything."

God used that ordeal to assure my heart of the greatness of His forgiveness toward me. He, like my earthly father, has already written the check for our forgiveness. The check is written with the ink of the blood of Christ. God has paid the penalty for the sins we are guilty of committing so that we might enter the adventure He has for us. He wants our fellowship. He does not want anything standing in the way of our relationship with Him.

You Are God's Treasure

I have a friend who loves junkyards, thrift stores, and garage sales. Her house is filled with the most amazing treasures. She has this incredible ability to see the hidden worth in cast-off, worn, and broken things. Once she acquires the desired object, she sets to work cleaning, polishing, painting, repairing, and even reupholstering. Every object in her house is a museum piece. There is something new and unique to see every time I visit. I love it.

In the same way, God scours the junkyards, thrift stores, and garage sales of this world looking for the castoffs. He has an eye for unique treasures. He purchases the articles He wants through the blood of His Son. He then sets to work restoring and renovating those rare pieces and turning each one into a showpiece for His glory. His grace transforms every flaw, every crack, every unusable part into a whole and beautiful work of His hands.

This truth is clearly evident in Ephesians 2:10: "We are His workmanship, created in Christ Jesus for good works, which God prepared beforehand that we should walk in them."

The truth is that God still has wonderful purposes for you. He wants to raise you from insignificance to significance by His glorious work in you. His work begins in you as you pray, believe, and obey His Word. Why not try it?

Questions for Study and Personal Reflection

1. Is there anything you've done or thought that you don't think God can forgive? Why do you hold onto this particular transgression?

   _____

   _____

   _____

   _____

2. What holds you back from believing God can forgive you?

   _____

   _____

_____

_____

3. How have your past failures or hurts impacted your ability to believe in God's grace?

_____

_____

_____

_____

4. Write out Romans 6:23 and answer the following questions.

_____

_____

_____

_____

What is the difference between a wage and a gift?

_____

_____

Which is God offering to you—a wage or a gift?

_____

_____

_____

How do you accept a gift?

_____

_____

_____

What is the gift that God is offering you?

_____

_____

_____

How can you receive His grace ?

_____

_____

_____

5. Write out below the sin(s) that you have struggled to forgive yourself for. Now use a pen with red ink to cross them out, reckoning them to be covered by the effectual blood of Jesus.

_____

_____

_____

_____

6. Write out a prayer to God thanking Him for forgiveness and asking Him to work through you and your weaknesses in a special and mighty way.

_____

_____

_____

_____

_____

Chapter 9

Lie: I Have Nothing to Offer

Have you heard, held, or lived the lie "I am insignificant. I have nothing to offer"?

Honestly, there is so much pressure these days to have some extraordinary talent, beauty, or accomplishment. Most women feel dwarfed by the images bombarding them every day at the market check stands. There on racks are the bold, the beautiful, and the accomplished. By contrast, the reality is the wife, mother, grandmother, single woman...ten pounds overweight, wearing whatever was clean in her closet, her hair disheveled, and her cart filled with frozen entrees. It's enough to make anyone feel belittled.

Have you been treated at times as if you were less important to God because you are a woman? Have you felt that others tried to cast you down? Have you felt an inner voice of condemnation that led you to believe you were less profitable to Him because of something you did? If so, you and I both need to explore the glory of our creation in Him and the power of resurrection in our lives through Christ.

Satan's lies are meant to make us inactive for the cause of God, so get busy and serve Jesus. Pray and ask God to show you what ministry He would have you involved in. Serving Jesus gets your mind off of yourself and your desires. I have found the best remedy to impatience is to get busy doing whatever God has set before me.

Did Eve Ever Wonder What to Do?

I have often wondered if Eve felt insignificant in the garden. Everything was taken care of. There was no need to water the plants, feed the animals, or prune the bushes. God took care of everything.

Adam had already named all the animals, so there was no need for her suggestions or creative skills.

Her husband had been created first. Maybe she felt, at times, like an afterthought rather than a gifted companion. All this is of course conjecture. Yet, the feeling of insignificance has caused more than one woman to bite into the forbidden.

One woman I interviewed, Addie, outlined her dissension into the forbidden. She kept trying to do good only to fail miserably at it. It seemed, to her mind, that everyone else was better at doing anything she attempted. "If I couldn't be good at something, I decided to be bad at everything!" This mindset compelled her into a life of self-destructive behavior that wasn't arrested until she received Jesus as her Savior.

Only after she was saved did she begin to realize the latent gifts that God had given her. She tapped into the wealth of ability simply by volunteering for whatever was needed. "I explained to the Christian women I met that I wasn't good at anything. They took me on board anyway." These Christian women assigned her one task after another.

Addie remembers directing quick prayers to God before attempting any of her assignments. Amazingly, she was able to do it. Soon she was volunteering for all sorts of ministries. She joined the women's ministry and became a group leader. Later she offered her services to a Christian radio ministry. With each new venture, Addie found she had more talents than she had ever realized.

We Forget to Ask

Some women go years caught in the lie of insignificance because even though they've prayed for their circumstances to change or prayed through the hard days of depression or sadness, they have forgotten to ask for direction toward their purpose. Don't forget to ask and then watch for God's leading in your life. When we go through seasons of our existence caught in questions about who we are and what we should be doing…be sure you're actually *asking God* the questions.

> Get busy serving Jesus! You will not only strengthen
> your resolve to resist the devil, but you
> will experience a sense of divine
> fulfillment as you work.

I have a friend who felt like she had nothing to offer the Lord by way of service. As she prayed and asked Him to give her some tangible way to serve Him, she remembered her mother's enchilada recipe. She volunteered to make them for every event and speaker that shared at our church. The enchiladas were greatly enjoyed.

Soon the Lord led her to volunteer for the worship team. Then she started teaching Sunday school. Presently, she oversees a prison ministry. You might say she started with one enchilada and now God has given her the whole enchilada!

Place yourself on the altar of God. Paul states it this way in Romans 6:13:

Do not present your members as instruments of unrighteousness to sin, but present yourselves to God as being alive from the dead, and your members as instruments of righteousness to God.

There are times when the devil tries to lie to me and tell me that I don't belong to Jesus. Whenever I hear that lie, I begin dedicating every part of myself to the Lord. I begin with my scalp and move all the way to the tip of my toes as I give every part of me to Jesus.

So get busy serving Jesus! You will not only strengthen your resolve to resist the devil, but you will experience a sense of divine fulfillment as you work.

The Power of the Lie

Where does the lie "I am insignificant" get its power? I think it has something to do with women being the weaker vessel (1 Peter 3:7). As women we struggle to loosen the lids of jars. We also have a tendency to concentrate on what we can't do rather than what we can do:

- We usually can't change someone's mind.

- We often can't make a grumpy teenager happy.

- We can't always please our husbands.

- We can't keep the house immaculately clean all the time.

- We can't change the world.

- We can't stop every injustice.

- We can't free the world from tyranny.

- We can't cure sickness.

- We can't always protect those we love from harm.

- We can't always be energetic, alert, attentive, and perfect!

We think of the things we can't do to the exclusion of the greatest things we can do:

- We can pray.
- We can believe God's Word.
- We can obey what the Bible says.

Because we don't see the immediate reward of praying, believing, and obeying, we often downplay their power. We often feel powerless. Yet, as women, we have infinite power at our disposal. We have the sovereign God of heaven listening to our prayers and waiting to bring His power to bear in every situation that we encounter. He will meet us with the answer, the directive, and the power to change what we can't do in our own strength.

What Are You Waiting For?

Do you believe this, my friend? You have something so wonderful to offer. Your gifting might be latent within you, just waiting to be discovered. On the other hand, you might train for something you never considered before and by the simple exercise of that thing, get strong in it. You will never know until you step out.

I was talking to a group of college freshmen a few weeks ago. I quizzed each young woman about her major and what she was hoping to do when she graduated. The girls confided to me that they felt overwhelmed. They were being required, in their mind, to make decisions that would affect them lifelong when they still weren't sure of their own likes and dislikes.

I totally agreed. I explained to them how I have lived in my present house for nine years and still haven't even painted my bedroom walls. I simply can't decide what color I want to wake up to every morning. So the walls remain covered with only their original base coat. Like the girls, I am afraid that I might do something that I become frustrated with.

A woman I know named Linda said she wanted to be a part of the women's ministry. Yet she turned down every position and service she was offered. Frustrated, one of the women asked her, "What are you waiting for?"

Linda thought for a moment. "I am waiting to feel it."

"Honey," the woman answered, "you won't feel it until you are doing it."

Are you waiting to feel it? Don't. Instead look for the opportunity to serve in whatever capacity you can right now. Look for opportunities to use your gifts and abilities and blessings.

Let Go of Insignificance—Embrace God's Purpose

God never meant for women to feel insignificant. From the very beginning, He had great plans for His unique creation. Even after the fall of Eve, He still had purposes for women. The women who discovered those purposes were the ones who believed and obeyed His Word.

We started our journey of letting go of lies by visiting the garden and by looking at the life of Eve, *not* because she is the cause of all of our problems, but rather because her temptation, sin, and shame reflect back to us how we respond to Satan's lies.

I was never more aware of the fact that we, as women, are all descendants of Eve and therefore susceptible to the same destructive lies as when I spoke with a group of young women and discovered the hurts they were carrying at such a young age.

I looked over my class of college students who had just studied the life of Eve. I asked the young women, "What lies have you heard lately?" Hands shot up everywhere. The class was rather large, and I knew this would take some time, but I also knew this was going to be a very important lesson for all of us.

I looked at Jilly. She was at the end of the front row and to my right. Her eyes looked around anxiously as she stated, "I will never get married." All around the class the other girls responded. "That's what I heard too," one said. Another shouted, "I heard that one right before I met my husband." We all laughed.

I smiled back at Jilly. "I'm glad you realize that's a lie. I heard that one too when I was in college."

As I polled the girls and heard the deceptions that they were tormented by, it hit me that I was not the only one who had been lied to. Feeling the sting of lies was a universal experience. My exposure to Satan's falsehoods was not a private thing. And my daily struggles with the troubles that follow misdirected belief was not my experience *just* because I had lived longer and had more time to feel the sharp barbs of dissatisfaction, sadness, discouragement, or the trials of life. We were all in this situation together. Satan was whispering in the ears of all these beautiful and vulnerable young women.

The girls continued. Some cried as they voiced the lies that had been altering their lives and faith for years: "I'm not valuable." "I'm not smart." "I won't do anything important with my life." "I'm only as good as the guy I'm dating or the job I'm doing." "God doesn't care about my self-fulfillment." "My failures are all people see." "Jesus hasn't forgiven me all my sins. There are still some sins I have to atone for."

As much as I wanted to let the girls share without interruption, by this time I couldn't help myself. I knew that these were not mere passing thoughts or comments the girls were repeating to me. These deceptions were becoming sources of great pain and profound damage. I couldn't let the devil lie to these precious daughters of the King anymore. We started to discuss God's truths and promises and how they countered, covered, and healed each and every one of these lies when we take on the protective knowledge of His Word.

Ephesians 6:16 mentions the "fiery darts of the wicked one" which only the "shield of faith" can extinguish. Certainly these lies were of the fiery-dart variety, and they were piercing holes in the faith of these young women. They had wounds in their vulnerable hearts and spirits because of these lies.

That day we all learned the value of the shield of faith. The shield of faith is the truth about God and what He has done and what He will do in and through our lives when we seek Him. As we hold up the truth of who God is and what He has promised to us as believers in Jesus, the darts of the enemy are quenched and their target is missed.

If only Eve had known about the shield of faith in the garden. She was vulnerable to the propaganda of the enemy because she did not have a strong grip on what God offered her in the safety of His will.

Satan had begun his seduction by eroding her faith in what God had said to her. He was piercing her confidence in the Creator. Now, without assurance in the Word of God, Eve was completely vulnerable to every falsehood from the devil.

In our class, as each falsehood was brought to the surface and met with the Word of Truth, the girls began to laugh. Satan was losing his grip on their thoughts. God was setting His girls free to embrace their identities in Christ and to become the women of purpose He designed them to be.

What You Do Matters

When I was pregnant, I visited a new hair salon for a bit of pampering and refreshment. The owner was very stylish. As she washed, cut, and styled my hair we talked. "I can't believe you're pregnant. You are so brave!" she exclaimed. "I never want to have children. It's too much pressure. I would want to dress them in designer clothes, get them the best education, and make sure they were all successful. I would go broke and have a nervous breakdown."

I smiled. "That's not my philosophy at all. I want my children to be loving individuals who are kind to others." I went on to explain that as a Christian, I hoped my kids would love God and those He created. I wanted my children to see the value in every human being.

"Wow! I never thought of it that way!" she said. Then she asked me if the child I was carrying was my first. Imagine her shock when I told her it was my fourth!

> Don't ever give yourself over to feeling
> "less than" another person.

I had entered that salon feeling a bit dowdy and out of sorts. And when I saw the stylish owner, I think my feelings of insignificance dropped me another level lower. However, as I started to share about what mattered to me and what mattered to God, I got excited. I felt confident, happy, and truly blessed. And do you know what? I think the stylist saw that in me. Not because of a new cut or a decision to go for bangs or no bangs, but because the desire to walk in God's purpose was very evident.

Realize that when you take steps toward becoming the woman God created you to be, you are attractive, significant, and you have much to offer. Don't ever give yourself over to feeling "less than" another person. And on the other side of that coin, always encourage someone else to feel their value. Point out the importance that comes with their unique purpose! Build them up in their search for God and meaning and fulfillment through faith.

What's in Your House?

Sometimes, as women, we don't see the significance in the talents we already have. We mistakenly think, *How could God ever use this?*

The woman mentioned in 2 Kings 4 had a dilemma. The creditors were coming to take possession of her boys. She went to the prophet Elisha begging for his help. Elisha asked her, "What do you have in your house?"

The woman replied, "Your maidservant has nothing in the house but a jar of oil." Elisha instructed her to collect all the vessels in her house and borrow as many other vessels as she could. She was then to go into her house with her sons, shutting the door behind her, and pour the oil into all the collected vessels.

The woman did as the prophet instructed. Vessel after vessel was filled from the insignificant little jar of oil. Soon she and her sons ran out of vessels to fill. She returned to the prophet, who told her to sell the oil, pay off the creditor, and live with her sons off of the proceeds.

There might be something in your life that you have overlooked. Some gift, some hobby, some passion that appears to you to be of no worth. Why not give that gift to God and see what He will do with it?

My mother-in-law, Carol, has never felt very useful to God, and yet she is one of the most productive women I know. Years ago she simply volunteered at her church. She began with the handicapped ministry. She pushed wheelchairs, befriended the enfeebled, and kept wipes handy for any mishaps. She thought nothing of her services.

Later she heard of a ministry that gave blankets to unwed mothers for their babies. Carol loves to sew. She has made each one of my children treasured blankets. She put her sewing skills to use making blankets for newborn babies.

After retirement, Carol learned that the bookstore at her church needed a volunteer. She had worked for over 40 years as an accountant. She brought her services to the church bookstore and became much appreciated.

Is there a little jar of oil in your house? I would venture to say that there are skills, talents, and giftings in your life that have been discounted. Make yourself and all you have available to God and see what He will do with your jar of oil.

What Gift Awaits Discovery?

When Brian and I lived in Vista, California, there were talented women who made centerpieces, decorated stages, and found gifts for the women who came to the retreats. I came to rely on the giftedness of these women. When we moved to England, there were no gifted women in sight to help with the centerpieces, stage decorations, and gifts for our first women's retreat. I was left to myself. With the excuse that I was desperate, I enlisted the help of some women who felt totally untalented.

Shopping one day, I found some mirrors that, with a little help, would make great centerpieces. Then I found some inexpensive silk flowers. Pulling out my glue gun I began to paste the flowers to the mirror. Voilà—a beautiful centerpiece! I told my helpers to do the same. They did and the mirrors looked gorgeous.

A friend from the States had sent me some embellished note

cards. I showed it to the women helping me. "We can do this," I said with a feigned tone of confidence ringing in my voice. Immediately we set to work. Within hours we had beautiful centerpieces and 100 gifts for the women who were signed up for the retreat.

"I have never done anything like this before," Jenny said, examining her work with admiration. "Me either," echoed Debbie.

These women became excited about the things God could and would do through them.

When Emptiness Is Abundance

At another retreat recently, I harnessed a friend, Lolly, to be my partner in laying hands on the women who came forward and praying for them. The needs of the women that came forward were tremendous. The first woman's kidneys were failing. She was angry with God for her poor health. I placed my hands on her shoulders and had Lolly lay a hand on her arm. I began to pray asking God to touch this precious woman with His power and understanding.

The next woman we prayed for was in dire straits. Her oldest son was in jail. Her second son was hyperactive, and her youngest son was autistic. Adding to her burden was the fact that her husband had recently abandoned the family. Again I placed my hands on this woman's shoulders and began to pray. When I finished the woman looked radiant.

I looked over at Lolly. She looked weak. Tears were pouring down her face. "Are you okay?" I whispered. She shook her head no.

Before I could attend to Lolly, another woman came forward. I recognized this young woman. Her husband had only recently been diagnosed with brain cancer. Again I placed my hands on her shoulders and began to pray.

After praying for a number of women, Lolly and I went to our rooms. On the walk to the lodge, she asked me, "How do you do it? I mean how do you pray for those women?"

"I just pray. I can't do anything for them, but Jesus can. He is just looking for an empty vessel. I can do empty."

"'I can do empty'?" Lolly repeated, astounded at the concept.

I went on to explain that God wanted to touch those women. I have nothing in myself to offer them. I don't have a doctor's skills. I don't have the diagnostic talents of a psychologist. I have no specialized training in working with women. However, I have Jesus, and He is more than enough.

God isn't looking for talent. He is looking for empty. He has more than enough talent to get the job done. He just needs a conduit that He can flow through. He needs you to say "I'm ready, Lord. I'm ready to be significant as Your woman."

I often think of Peter and John going to the temple in Acts 3. As they enter, a lame man asks them for alms. Peter fixes his eyes on the man and says, "Silver and gold I do not have, but what I do have I give you: In the name of Jesus Christ of Nazareth, rise up and walk." Peter then took the man by the hand and raised him to his feet. Immediately the man began to walk, leap, and praise God.

What would have happened if Peter had had gold and silver to give the lame man? The lame man would have died a lame man. He never would have experienced the power of God surging throughout his limbs.

You don't need silver and gold to be a conduit for God. You simply need to be empty and available. He wants women who will find all they need in Him. He wants to flow through women and bless them with His power.

You have gifting through Jesus. You have something to offer to

God. Do you know what it is? You can offer your life as an empty vessel waiting for His filling.

Can you "do empty"? Ask God to fill you with His grace. You will never know what He desires to do through you until you make yourself available to Him.

So, whether you face something you already know how to do or something that you have never done before, God desires to use you for His glory. Simply make yourself available. Look for opportunities in your church, community, family, and even neighborhood. You will never feel it until you do it.

Questions for Study and Personal Reflection

1. Spend time reading this passage written by Paul:

> *Each time he said, "My grace is all you need. My power works best in weakness." So now I am glad to boast about my weaknesses, so that the power of Christ can work through me. That's why I take pleasure in my weaknesses, and in the insults, hardships, persecutions, and troubles that I suffer for Christ. For when I am weak, then I am strong (2 Corinthians 12:9 NLT).*

    a. How might taking pleasure in your weaknesses bring you freedom?

_____

_____

_____

_____

b. How does this amazing truth shed light on your life?

_____

_____

_____

_____

2. Make a list of the areas of life in which you feel insufficient. How do you think God might be revealing His grace and strength through you in those areas?

_____

_____

_____

_____

_____

3. Now make a list of the things you feel are your gifts. Write down how you can offer these talents to God for His service. Which parts of yourself and which abilities have you held back from surrendering to Him?

_____

_____

_____

_____

_____

4. Read Acts 3:1-11. What amazing things happened because Peter and John were lacking silver and gold?

_____

_____

_____

_____

_____

5. How have you shortchanged your service to the Lord by believing that you didn't have the ability or value to serve Him? Describe how good it will feel to lean on His strength to work in and through you to accomplish great things to honor Him.

_____

_____

_____

_____

Chapter 10

Lie: I Can Do This Without God

Doing only what you want to do can be a dangerous thing. If I only did what I wanted to, I'd eat chocolate and donuts and never eat vegetables and protein. Now where would that leave me?

While I do advocate *some* self-consideration, Satan enticed Eve to focus solely on herself. He distracted her from considering the consequences of her actions. It was no longer about what God said, or what God wanted, or what was best for Adam—it was about what Eve wanted. Through self-focus an insatiable hunger was conceived for self-gratification to the exclusion of God's Word or God's will. She might have reasoned, *If God didn't want me to eat of the tree, why did He put it in the garden?*

Perhaps this is a line of reasoning you have heard before. *If God doesn't want me to sin, why doesn't He take the desire for sin away?* He allows temptations to give us the opportunity to choose His will above our own. In this way we have the chance to show Him how much we love Him.

Temptations also give us the opportunity to grow stronger in our resolve to obey. The more we resist a temptation, the less power it has to sway and allure us.

Finally, God does not take away the forbidden because the forbidden reveals to us the true nature of our heart. If we didn't have the forbidden, we would think we were great people. We would never know the cravings of our fallen nature and our need of a righteous Savior.

The "Me First" Attitude Always Loses

While I was on a recent round of shopping at a health-food store, a woman rudely cut in front of me. She nearly slammed into my cart. When we crossed paths again an aisle later, I got a good look at her. She wore a sweatshirt that read, "It's all about me!" I think she not only believed that slogan but lived it out.

Do some of us live like this? We might not wear the sweatshirt, but we might be wearing the attitude out in the open. Unchecked desire can lead to selfish ambition. Selfish ambition leads to sin. Sin is doing what God has forbidden. Eve did not set out to disobey God. She observed and respected the prohibition to not "eat" of the tree of the knowledge of good and evil until her desire became fixed on its fruit. Before that time she had not even considered breaking God's command.

Eve became so fixated on her desire to eat the tantalizing fruit that she began to believe Satan's lies and question God's command: Did God really say she couldn't eat of this tree in the garden? Certainly she couldn't die from just one bite! Was God's prohibition simply to keep her from becoming like Him?

> Sin is the outcome of unchecked desire and selfish ambition…We sin when we try to fulfill our desires with our own schemes and plans.

Jen never thought she would have an abortion. She loved babies and kids. The idea of an abortion was totally repulsive to her. But that was all before she met Eddie. She was attracted to him from the first moment she saw him. There was an air of intrigue to him. He was handsome and reckless. She thought about him all the time.

Eddie was not a Christian. Jen had been raised in a Christian home. Eddie was everything her parents had warned her about. But she was smitten. In her mind she made up all sorts of scenarios about him. She was sure that she could reform him.

Jen actively pursued Eddie. She flirted with him and even asked him out. After a time they were dating. When she told him she was pregnant, he told her that he wanted nothing to do with her or the baby. Then he left town.

Jen was afraid to tell her parents. They had warned her over and over again about Eddie. Scared and heartbroken, she visited the abortion clinic. Waking up from the anesthesia, she wept. She couldn't believe what she had done. Her life spiraled downward after that. She got involved with drugs, alcohol, and a promiscuous lifestyle. Every attempt by her parents to lead her back to Jesus was rebuffed.

Then one day, after having her second abortion, Jen was at the end. This time, when her brother called, she listened to the message about the love and forgiveness of Jesus.

"I was the last person to have an abortion. Then I had two," Jen confided in me one day. "It all started with my determination to capture Eddie's heart and keep it. In the end, I lost Eddie, a part of myself, and our baby too."

Sin is the outcome of unchecked desire and selfish ambition. Like Eve, rarely does someone set out to sin. We sin when we try to fulfill our desires with our own schemes and plans. We sin when we try to live our lives in our power and not in God's strength.

Ignoring God

Sadly, there are many, many stories of women ignoring God's truths. I believe that once women start down a path of thinking that they don't deserve God's love, they also start down the path of trying to do things in their own power. It's a combination of brokenness and pride, and it can destroy lives.

Rhoda is a blonde-haired beauty. Everything about her bearing reminds you of a beach girl. She has a big beautiful smile, sparkling blue eyes, and a laid-back disposition.

Rhoda was ecstatic when she was accepted to Bible college. She couldn't wait to solidify her faith in Christ through intensive study of God's Word. Though she started with a single focus, there was another student who soon grasped her attention. Blake purposely sat near her in their classes. He asked to borrow her notes on more than one occasion. They talked infrequently, but she couldn't help noticing how attractive he was.

As they chatted one day, he suddenly proposed to her. Rhoda was taken by surprise but excited. Without thinking or praying about it she said, "Yes." She reasoned there was nothing to pray about, really. Even though she hardly knew Blake, he, like herself, was a student at the Bible college. She reasoned that he must have the same pursuit that she did, to know and serve the Lord.

They were married within the month. It turned out that Blake was withdrawn and moody. He demanded his own private time. He would spend hours alone with his computer. Rhoda tried in vain to draw him out of his cocoon. One day, when he was gone, she opened his computer. On the screen appeared vivid and perverse images of sexual pornography. Rhoda felt ill. She ran to the bathroom and threw up.

When Blake came home she confronted him. His face immediately reddened and a torrent of verbal abuse spewed from his mouth. He grabbed her and violently threw her to the ground.

Rhoda made plans to leave and have the marriage annulled, but Blake found her and apologized profusely. He promised that he was through with the pornography and would never treat her harshly again. She looked at his handsome face and forgave him.

He suggested a new start, and Rhoda agreed. She desperately wanted this marriage to work. She was embarrassed that she had acted so impulsively in marrying him. She wanted to prove to herself and others that it was the right decision.

The move proved to be a terrible mistake. Blake's behavior grew more aggressive, and she finally had to flee for her life.

I met up with Rhoda after the collapse of her marriage. She was condemned and confused. She couldn't come to terms with the fact that Blake had claimed to be a Christian and had gone to Bible college, but now he didn't show any interest in seeking God's guidance or forgiveness. I explained to her about Satan's presence in the garden. "Satan met up with you at the garden of Bible college. In Eden he disguised himself as a serpent—here, at Bible college, he disguised himself as a student."

Rhoda admitted to rushing past all the warning signs. She loved the thrill of venturing out into the unknown. Marrying someone she barely knew had an air of mystery and romance that she had only read about in romantic novels. The reality was a stark contrast to the happy endings of the fictional stories she had read.

Why Do You Go It Alone?

When Satan promised Eve, "You will be like God, knowing good and evil," he was advocating godlikeness through rebellion. There is a huge movement today of people proclaiming themselves to be their own god. One actress recounted in her autobiography how she stood on the beach and screamed toward heaven, "I am God!"

Selfish ambition follows unchecked desire. If we do not submit our desires to God, like Eve our desires can become corrupted. Satan will lie to us, as he did to her, and tell us that the only way to fulfill our desire is through disobedience to God's ways. He will convince us that God will not fulfill our desire, so we must do it for ourselves.

Selfish ambition does not consider the effect our actions will have on others. It is preoccupied with the fulfillment of desire and fulfilling ourselves. Selfish ambition is using any way readily available to us in order to get our desires fulfilled. We have all heard the saying "The end justifies the means." This type of reasoning has caused immense suffering and mayhem in families, communities, and around the world. Many innocent people have been hurt because of the selfish aims of a few individuals.

Years ago I was appalled to read about a mother who hired a hit man to harm two other girls who were competing with her daughter for a spot on the cheer team. The mother's ambition for her daughter was at the expense of two young girls.

James 3:16 says, "Where envy and self-seeking exist, confusion and every evil thing are there." You can be sure Satan is behind every selfish ambition that whispers, *Do it for yourself!*

It's hard to wait for the fulfillment of a desire, even a good desire. Satan is waiting to take advantage of that desire to corrupt it or turn it into selfish ambition. We are so used to instant gratification that the idea of waiting seems tortuous.

The other day, I visited a drive-through restaurant. At the window I noticed a digital timer. I asked the clerk what it was for. She responded, "If we don't get your order to you in four minutes or less, your order is free!"

Just hours later, I heard the manager at my favorite coffee shop training a recruit. "You have to pop those drinks out within three minutes. No one wants to wait over five minutes for their coffee."

No, we don't like to wait. We don't like to wait for food, coffee, a thirst quencher, an outfit, a ride, or to buy our groceries. We want immediate fulfillment of all our desires.

Not only do we want immediate fulfillment, we also want the easiest way to fulfill those desires. We don't want anything that takes sacrifice on our part. Con artists know this about our nature. They offer investments that promise great gains with very little effort or financial commitment on the part of the investor. They offer fast and easy money. The reality is, there are no fast and easy investments.

God is not unmindful of our desires. He wants to give us the desires of our heart. He wants to keep those desires pure. In the process of fulfilling those desires He wants to teach us rich and timeless lessons. He also wants to work out those desires in His divine way, at the divine time, and without our interference.

When you hear a fast and easy answer to your desires, beware. I can't tell you the countless times Satan has whispered to me. It might be a situation concerning a person I want corrected. Now correction is a good desire, right? But when I hear a voice whispering to me to take it over and do it myself or take matters into my own hands, I know that the devil is trying to get into my head. I stop immediately and give that thought over to God and ask Him to accomplish His will, His way, in His perfect time.

No, I don't like to wait, but I have learned the truth of Isaiah 49:23: "They shall not be ashamed who wait for Me." I have had a few too many experiences of doing things my way and paying a higher price later. There has never been a time when I gave someone a piece of my mind that I didn't wish that I had that piece back! Honestly, the times in my past that I am most ashamed of are the times where I took things into my own hands without waiting on the Lord.

Whenever we set out to quickly fulfill our own desires with little self-sacrifice we have entered the dangerous field of self-ambition.

Let Go of Pride—Embrace Trust

Here's a true confession. I used to be a very messy house-wife. I just couldn't get a handle on all the household chores. The demands of being a young pastor's wife, fulfilling my creative energies, and taking care of my two toddlers left me with little time to maintain the upkeep of the house. The minute I finished straightening, cleaning, dusting, and folding the clothes, the toys would begin to creep out of the closets and the dust bunnies would hold a bunny vigil in every corner of my house.

One day, at a small Bible study for women, I shared my frustrations and asked for prayer. Another woman in the group smiled at me and said, "I used to be right where you are at." Then she gave me some great advice.

I looked at her wondering what great solution she was going to offer me. The woman challenged me to read Proverbs 31:10-33 every day. She told me that after she added those verses to her daily reading, her housework became effortless.

I restrained myself from rolling my eyes and gave a forced smile. Trying to sound as sincere as possible I uttered a thank-you. *Ridiculous*, I thought. The truth is that I was stubborn and prideful. I basically felt that this everyday issue was something that I should be able to resolve on my own without outside advice from others or help from God. Mostly, I felt embarrassed that this was an issue for me. Why couldn't I handle the management of my own home? Didn't women do this every day?

> I don't believe in magic formulas, but…God's Word
> has the ability to work in us in unimaginable ways.

A couple of days later I entered the house after an afternoon of running errands. I was, once again, overwhelmed by the magnitude of the job before me. Something in me decided to give the Proverbs 31 reading a try.

While the kids climbed over the furniture and knocked the cushions off, I read about this perfect biblical woman who had it all together. She even got to go shopping and buy imported goods. Rather than feeling inspired, I was intimidated. Nevertheless, I added this passage in Proverbs to my daily reading.

I can't explain how it happened, but it did. The housework seemed to get easier. A friend showed me how she kept a basket in every room and at the end of the day threw all her kids' toys in it. It helped to keep the room neat. Later she would sort and put the items away. I got baskets for every room.

Another friend told me she started every morning with one load of laundry. I started doing a load every morning. I learned a few other tricks along the way for keeping up with my housecleaning. The next thing I knew, the house stayed clean and picked up. I thought about my daily reading. Ever since I had added the testimony of the Proverbs 31 woman, housework had gotten easier. I don't believe in magic formulas, but I believe I was affected by the testimony of this biblical woman. God's Word has the ability to work in us in unimaginable ways.

God Is So Much Bigger than Your Weakness

As I was walking the other day, I was praying about a particularly hard situation. I felt the Lord prompting my heart. *Cheryl, look at the sky.* I looked up at the vast violet-blue expanse overhead.

Next I felt the Lord say, *Now look at the trees around you.* I looked at various trees of all sizes, with their variegated and unique leaves. Some bent low to the earth, while others reached toward the sky with their bulging branches. A flock of finches flew within a few feet of my path. *Cheryl, can you make a sky? Would you even think of the concept? Do you know the chemical composition that makes it look like crystal? Can you create a tree? Can you curve its branches and send nourishment to its leaves through the nitrogen in the soil? What about the birds? Can you instruct them on how to fly or find them nesting places?* I almost laughed out loud as I answered each question with a definite no. *Then let Me handle it,* was the answer that reverberated from heaven.

God has many responsibilities. The thought that we, in our finite state, can assume His position is folly. The thought that His divine will should be subject to our finite whims is ludicrous. The idea of godlikeness, power, and control are enticing, especially in a world that seems to be careening out of control. But the truth is that man cannot achieve any form of godlikeness apart from God.

The godlikeness man really longs for is offered through Jesus Christ alone. Jesus promised to anyone who would receive Him the authority to become the children of God (John 1:12). In 2 Peter 1:4, Peter states that God has given us "exceedingly great and precious promises, that through these you may be partakers of the divine nature, having escaped the corruption that is in the world through lust."

Jesus alone imparts the "divine nature" of God to us. It is through Him that we can acquire access to the throne of God (Hebrews 4:16). It is the person of Jesus taking residency in us that brings divinity to our lives. Apart from Him we do not have anything that even begins to approach the wisdom and magnificence of God.

Mankind needs a God who is greater than he is. We need a God who is more powerful than any man, army, or force on earth. We need a God whose wisdom holds the universe in check and regulates all the matters of earth. We need a God whose tender mercies are innumerable and renewed every morning. We need a God who is above corruption. We need a God who is so aware of His creation that He knows the number of hairs on every scalp. We need the God of the Bible.

In Your Weakness, He Is Strong

In Romans 12:1, the apostle Paul urged his readers to present their bodies to God as a living sacrifice, holy and acceptable to Him. Paul understood that God wasn't asking for talents, resources, or accomplishments but for lives of men and women.

Though the apostle Paul wrote the majority of the epistles in the New Testament, established prominent churches throughout the Roman Empire, and preached to the Greek intellectuals on Mars Hill, he felt insufficient. Yet he was called to take the gospel of Christ to the sophisticated pagan world of Greeks and Romans. In speaking of this call, Paul wrote, "And who is sufficient for these things?" (2 Corinthians 2:16).

By Paul's own admission he was sickly, his Greek was unsophisticated, and he often trembled publicly. Yet he did not allow these inadequacies to stop him. He tapped into a superior source of strength that allowed him to do the unimaginable. He tapped into God's grace.

In 2 Corinthians 12, Paul recounts his encounter with God's grace. For years he had suffered with a chronic ailment he described as "a messenger of Satan to buffet him." At times, he felt crippled by this affliction. He pleaded with God on three specific occasions to deliver him from it. Imagine that! The apostle Paul, who prayed for others and saw them healed and delivered, was not delivered from his own affliction when he prayed. Rather, God answered his prayer by telling him, "My grace is sufficient for you, for My strength is made perfect in weakness" (2 Corinthians 12:9).

Paul learned that he didn't need to be strong or accomplished to do amazing works for God. He only needed to be available and willing. God desired to work, by His grace, through Paul.

We cannot ever attain God's power, but who would want to be responsible for keeping all the planets spinning and keeping their orbits in check? God in His infinite mercy promises to work His power in us. By letting go of our pride and false perceptions, we are able to receive His power and give Him glory through our honorable, selfless, and faithful lives.

Questions for Study and Personal Reflection

1. When have you tried to fulfill your desires instead of asking God to direct your heart and your actions? What happened?

　　_____

　　_____

　　_____

　　_____

2. Have you ever thought that doing things on your own is the same as wanting to "be" God? How does this perspective make you want to change the way you approach your decisions and actions?

　　_____

_____

_____

_____

3. Ask God to point out areas of life or specific circumstances
   where pride, stubbornness, or selfish ambitions interfere with
   His purpose and desires for you.

_____

_____

_____

_____

4. What are some ways that you can give yourself and your day
   to God?

_____

_____

_____

_____

5. Start your morning or close your day in God's Word. Select a
   passage that instructs you in a particular area of need right now.
   Write it down here and commit to memorizing it over the next
   week.

_____

_____

_____

6. Describe how it feels to release pride in exchange for God's purpose. Is it painful? Does it challenge you? Give your feelings to
   Him and enjoy His presence and peace.

   _____

   _____

   _____

   _____

Chapter 11

Lie: Just One Bite Won't Matter

I had been on my diet for over a week. Each time a sweet was offered, I refused with greater resolve. That was before the tantalizing plate of fudge brownies. "Oh, I can always diet tomorrow," I said before I scooped a brownie off the plate and sunk my teeth into the tempting square. Yuck! The brownies must have been at least a week old. They were dry and tasteless. There was even an aftertaste of something bitter.

Now I was mad. One week of sacrifice and exercise had just flown out the window for one of the worst taste and texture experiences I had ever had. Since I had already blown it, I decided to *really* blow it. I tried a bite of every treat that was offered to me. I figured it this way: *Today I will eat, drink, and be merry because tomorrow I diet!*

Nothing satisfied my sweet tooth. Everything I tried left me disappointed. I went to bed that night frustrated, angry with myself for breaking my diet and for devouring 2000 calories over the national daily average.

Isn't it funny how sometimes we are sure something is going to taste a certain way and it doesn't at all? I have never seen a dessert that didn't look delicious! Even those plastic desserts in the bakery section cases look good.

That's how the forbidden fruit looked to Eve. It looked like it was going to taste delicious. She was sure it was going to satisfy her. So she picked the fruit and ate it. Then she shared it with Adam. The outcome, like the bite of my brownie, was not what she expected.

Immediate Consequences

There were unforeseen consequences to Eve's actions. Those consequences were immediate and far-reaching. The first consequence was that her eyes were opened. She suddenly saw what she hadn't seen before. Where before she had only seen good, now she saw evil.

Sin has a way of opening our eyes to the darkest scenarios of life. It always results in the loss of innocence. It brings the darkness of distrust, disillusionment, and demoralization. Nothing is as it was. Things that once seemed innocent are shrouded in shadows.

Imagine Eve's shock when her eyes were opened and she realized she had been talking to the devil! Often that is the case—it is not until we've bitten down hard that we realize who has offered us the fruit.

Denise met Gary at church. By this time she was already very successful in her career and owned her own home. Gary also looked successful. He had a great job. He was handsome and appeared motivated. She was elated when he proposed after a few months of dating. However, something didn't seem right in the back of her mind. She loved what she knew of Gary, but there seemed to be a side to him that she didn't know at all.

....

She had enjoyed a few bites of…love? Lust? The thrill of being pursued? But then, she hadn't stopped to assess what God's leading was for her life's path.

....

Denise ignored her own misgivings and the concerns of friends and family about her marrying Gary. Immediately after the wedding, she knew something was wrong. He left her alone for hours on their honeymoon with no explanation of where he had been or what he had been doing. He criticized her constantly no matter what she did, wore, or said.

Three months into the marriage, Denise found evidence of the other women in Gary's life. When she confronted him, he admitted everything. He left the house. The following week, he sent her divorce papers. The marriage and divorce cost Denise her house, her savings and, for a time, her health.

She will readily admit that it wasn't until she said "I do" that she realized she had married someone completely different than the man she thought he was. She had enjoyed a few bites of…love? Lust? The thrill of being pursued? But then, she hadn't stopped to assess what God's leading was for her life's path.

A Moment of Weakness

I rarely watch television, so I am not quite sure what made me turn to it looking for answers and satisfaction. Nonetheless, it happened. I was doing housework, when I heard an infomercial host extolling the virtues of a fruit dehydrator. I stopped folding the clothes and gave the television my full attention. It wasn't long before I *knew* I needed what that man was selling. Though I had never seen a food dehydrator before, nor even considered owning one, the thought of living one more day without it seemed neglectful.

I called the number flashing on the screen and ordered one. In a few days a huge box arrived. With great anticipation I opened it. I began to flip through the instructions. They were overwhelming, to say the least, but I was determined.

I set out to buy all the ingredients I'd need to provide delicious, healthful, and economical treats for my family. Nothing turned out the way I planned. Don't get me wrong—I don't blame the infomercial, the recipes, or even the dehydrator. I blame myself.

The ingredients were costly. The procedure was complex. The cleanup was laborious. The dehydrated snacks looked unappetizing and didn't taste the way I thought they would. The kids hated the new snacks. In the end, I sold the whole contraption for less than five dollars at a garage sale.

What made me bite? It was the appeal of something new that would change everything. It was the promise of enhancing my diet and the diet of my children. It was the televised, tantalizing display of dried berries, bananas, and apples. I also think it had a little something to do with the fact that I was hungry when I was folding the clothes.

Like Eve, I had bitten down hard. It was a bad choice. I was lured away by my own desires and fantasies. I hadn't taken the time to consult Brian, or even the Lord for that matter. I had picked up the phone without thought and placed the order for the "life-changing" dehydrator.

Is buying a food dehydrator a bad thing? Will it be my downfall and spread sin throughout my life? No. Drying apples and beef to make snacks is not evil. However, if I had paused for even a moment, I would've realized that for me and for that time in our lives, it wasn't a wise choice to make. I completely bypassed my usual process of weighing a decision carefully and in light of my family's needs and God's best for us. That is the point where "Oh, why not" can turn into "I wish I hadn't."

Shopping is perhaps the most noticeable way that women give their decisions over to the power of temptation instead of to God's discernment. How many times have you made a "Why not?" purchase and then a day later, a week later—or maybe a month later when the Visa bill comes—it is definitely an "I wish I hadn't" decision?

These small regrets can be easily dismissed as we shake our head and wish we'd been wiser. However, these small decisions do add up to a pattern, a life behavior, and very possibly a major lie that undermines many aspects of a godly life, including godly steward-ship, obedience, patience, moderation, and selflessness.

Until the day when sin has been annihilated, we as believers need to be on guard lest Satan or anyone else should try to deceive us into thinking that sin does not have harmful consequences. Sin is never safe. The apostle Paul warned,

> *Do not be deceived, God is not mocked; for whatever a man sows, that he will also reap. For he who sows to his flesh will of the flesh reap corruption, but he who sows to the Spirit will of the Spirit reap everlasting life (Galatians 6:7-8).*

Nibbles of Regret

Every day, in a thousand different ways, Eve's fateful action is repeated by women. I myself have copied her folly a myriad of times. Just as there are false, "one-bite solutions" to our problems and times of discontentment, there are also seemingly harmless "first bites" of sinful behavior that can lead our hearts and minds down a slippery slope of anger, impatience, lies, and other paths of regret. Here are a few of those nibbles:

We take a bite when we get angry and lash out at someone.

We take a bite when we say an unkind word to someone.

We take a bite when we neglect our Bible.

We take a bite when we tell a lie.

We take a bite when we gossip.

We take a bite when we listen to slander.

We take a bite when we gossip about a sister or brother in the Lord.

We take a bite when we entertain fantasies in our mind.

We take a bite when we watch unedifying movies or read unprofitable books.

We take a bite when we fight with our friends.

We take a bite when we speed in our cars.

We take a bite when we complain.

We take a bite when we allow condemnation to get a foothold in our mind.

We take a bite when we refuse to forgive.

Where or how do you encounter your greatest temptations? Do your temptations seem to mostly be spiritual, physical, or emotional? We are each unique beings and creations. God shaped you and me differently. And often our patterns of want and temptation vary as well. But we do have things in common. Desires are inevitable and are a part of us. God even plants His desires in our hearts. It is the devil that wants to corrupt those good desires and prompt us to act in our own time, our own powers, and our own will. We can't avoid encountering temptation, but we do have the power to resist Eve's folly.

We must recognize what's in our hearts that makes us susceptible to lies and to enticements that lead us along ungodly paths. Jesus said,

Hear Me, everyone, and understand: There is nothing that enters a man from outside which can defile him; but the things

which come out of him, those are the things that defile a man...For from within, out of the heart of men, proceed evil thoughts, adulteries, fornications, murders, thefts, covetousness, wickedness, deceit, lewdness, an evil eye, blasphemy, pride, foolishness. All these evil things come from within and defile a man (Mark 7:14-15,21-23).

When vengeful, condemning, or selfish thoughts come to my mind or out of my mouth, I immediately examine my heart. It's not easy for me to identify a heart problem, so I present my heart to God. Jeremiah 17:9 asks, "The heart is deceitful above all things, and desperately wicked; who can know it?" The answer follows in verse 10, "I, the LORD, search the heart, I test the mind." God knows my heart. So when I get those unhealthy thoughts, I present my heart to Him for a heart check.

One of my dearest friends was going through a particularly hard time. She read Proverbs 4:23, which instructs, "Keep your heart with all diligence, for out of it spring the issues of life." As she read it, she cried out, "Lord, I am not strong enough to keep my own heart." She recognized the nature of her heart to react to the circumstances rather than to His promises.

She told me the Lord immediately comforted her with the knowledge found in 1 John 3:20, "If our heart condemns us, God is greater than our heart, and knows all things." God showed her that He could overpower and cleanse her heart. He would keep her heart for her.

What Makes Us Bite?

There are varied reasons why we bite. Something that tempts a friend to take a bite might not tempt us at all. We can easily be baffled by why Eve was so tempted by the fruit on the tree, and yet we find it quite understandable when we are unable to refuse an extra piece of fudge cake. The motivation to bite is different for each of us.

When Satan appears before the throne of God in Job 1, God asks Satan where he has been. His answer is frightening. "From going to and fro on the earth, and from walking back and forth on it" (Job 1:7).

It is obvious from Satan's next response to God that he had been scrutinizing God's servant Job. After God mentions this man, Satan says,

> *Does Job fear God for nothing? Have You not made a hedge around him, around his household, and around all that he has on every side? You have blessed the work of his hands, and his possessions have increased in the land. But now, stretch out Your hand and touch all that he has, and he will surely curse You to Your face! (Job 1:9-11).*

Satan had been studying Job to find an area of weakness. He was strategizing how to make Job take a bite. In Job's case the bite was to curse God.

First Peter 5:8 warns, "Be sober, be vigilant; because your adversary the devil walks about like a roaring lion, seeking whom he may devour." Satan roams the earth looking for victims. He studies the habits of men and women, looking for ways to tempt them to take a bite of the forbidden fruit. Our weaknesses become the perfect opening for our faith and integrity to be tempted and torn.

When Satan offers an immediate remedy to your situation, don't take that bite!

Let Go of Temptation—Embrace God's Strength

When Satan spoke to Eve, he was beguiling. He was intriguing. He was interesting. He didn't become adversarial and cause a huge conflict. That could send someone running. Instead, he woos a person. He entices and tempts. During his conversation with Eve, he inquired about her opinion and asked her how she felt about things in the garden. That's a hook for just about any woman! There is something so beguiling about someone being interested in our opinion.

If only Eve could have realized the nature and intent of the serpent that flattered her, things might have played out differently.

When Brian's and my first church in Vista, California, was just beginning to burst at the seams, an old crush of mine showed up at church. He met me at the door of the classroom where I was picking up my children from class. "Wow, they seem like a lot of work," he said. I replied that they were actually a delight.

> I walked away and felt the freedom that comes with surrendering even the smallest chance of temptation to God's certain hope and power.

He countered by asking me if I ever got any free time. "Does Brian ever take you out?" Distractedly I answered that we had been busy lately.

He asked me if Brian was still surfing. I replied that he was. "Does Brian ever take you surfing with him?"

"No."

"If you were my wife I would not only take you surfing but I would have you ride on my board with me." I actually laughed out loud. I recognized that potentially sinful behavior was being offered, and I wasn't about to take a bite.

I quickly excused myself and found solace in the company of Brian as he greeted the parishioners at the church door.

Had I let my ego become inflated by the flattery or allowed my thoughts to linger on questions about what Brian was or wasn't doing, I would've been taking a dangerous first bite. Even if that first bite had merely shifted me into a bad mood or turned my attitude toward Brian sour, it would've ruined a perfectly great day with my family. That one bite could have turned into a full buffet of dissatisfaction, but I walked away and felt the freedom that comes with surrendering even the smallest chance of temptation to God's certain hope and power.

Follow Truth Instead of Emotions

Satan focused Eve's attention on the forbidden and also on her emotions and her personal viewpoint. She had never thought much about how she felt about the prohibition that God placed on her and Adam to not eat of the one tree. Satan not only raised doubt about the validity of the prohibition, he asked how Eve felt about the restriction. It was a grand invitation to take a bite.

I remember having to leave a meeting early to go make dinner for Brian and the kids. "Does Brian make you cook dinner for him?" one of the women asked.

I answered affirmatively but added, "I like making dinner. I love to cook."

She looked dubious. "It just seems so unfair to me. How do you feel about making dinner? Wouldn't you rather he give you a break and take you out?"

Honestly, up until that time I had never thought about my emotional reaction to cooking dinner. It was something I did. All the way home in the car I was thinking about all the things involved in cooking dinner. There was the meal planning, the shopping, the sorting and storing of the food. There were the dishes and the preparations. It seemed like each step played out in my mind, and I was gauging my emotional response to each step, when I suddenly remembered the words of Jesus, "Let him deny himself, and take up his cross daily, and follow Me" (Luke 9:23).

I thought about how dangerous it would be to trust my initial emotional response, when it was clearly something that incited discontent. The one comment from the other woman could've whisked me away down the slippery slope of faulty thinking and then into the danger zone of questioning a priority I had set for myself and my family time.

Okay, so there is never a time I am deeply inspired to do the dishes. I never long to wash, dry, and fold clothes. So it wouldn't be difficult to leap from taking one bite of dissatisfaction to being all-out angry about my responsibilities. There are two risky lies surrounding sin or sinful behavior. The first lie is that one bite won't hurt. "I can entertain a little sin without any consequences." The second lie is "I've already sinned, so I might as well give myself fully to it." Both of these attitudes leave out spiritual discernment and God's best for our situation.

When we open our eyes to what is a lie or a temptation that's presented, we can then replace initial feelings of longing, pride, or dissatisfaction with God's desires for us, including humility, faithfulness, and wisdom. Don't let the first thread of your emotions get the best of you. You do have opportunities to make the great exchange of destructive temptations for godly desires.

Two Gardens, Two Responses

Two of the most important events in history took place in a garden. The first was the temptation and fall of Eve in the Garden of Eden. The even greater event took place in the Garden of Gethsemane.

In Eden, Eve was deceived by the devil's lies and motivated by her own desire to have more. In Gethsemane, Jesus resisted the

lies of the devil and the desire to save Himself and willingly submitted to His Father's will. In agony He prayed, "Not My will, but
Yours, be done" (Luke 22:42). Jesus knew the rejection, condemnation, and brutality that awaited Him. Hebrews 12:2 states that
He "endured the cross, despising the shame."

In the garden of Gethsemane He resolved, according to the will
and foreordained purpose of God, to endure the cross and bear the
sins of the world on His sinless frame.

In the perfect and beautiful Garden of Eden, Eve's decision led
to the curse of sin falling upon all men. In the rugged Garden of
Gethsemane Jesus resolved to provide salvation from the curse of
sin by sacrificing His sinless life for all men.

Adam and Eve were forbidden from reentering the Garden of
Eden and eating of the tree of life. Jesus, by His sacrificial death,
has again made the tree of life accessible to mankind (Revelation
22:14). He has promised that if anyone believes in Him they will
have everlasting life (John 3:16).

Through Eve both the curse of sin and the promise of a
redeemer came. God promised in Genesis 3:15 that through Eve's
seed, one would come who would bruise the head of Satan. Jesus
did this very thing when He died on the cross for the curse of sin.
Colossians 2:13-15 revels in this victory when it states,

> *You, being dead in your trespasses and the uncircumcision of
> your flesh, He has made alive together with Him, having forgiven
> you all trespasses, having wiped out the handwriting of require-
> ments that was against us, which was contrary to us. And He has
> taken it out of the way, having nailed it to the cross. Having dis-
> armed principalities and powers, He made a public spectacle of
> them, triumphing over them in it.*

Jesus bruised Satan's head upon the cross at Calvary.

His ultimate victory was realized in His resurrection from the dead. Now the living Savior offers forgiveness of sins, freedom from the devil's oppression, and the hope of the garden of heaven to all who will receive Him.

Through Jesus, though we have made the same choices as Eve, we have the forgiveness of our sins and access to the tree of life. Through Jesus, we have power over the enemy's lies and persuasions. We have a way to maneuver through our emotions, discern the lies from the truth, and claim the strength of the Lord as our foundation.

Resiste that one bite. It does matter. It will impact your life. Instead, feast on the Word of and love of God. Fill your heart's every need with the wonders of faith and commitment. This is the satisfied life you've always longed for.

Questions for Study and Personal Reflection

1. What makes you bite when you encounter temptations?

_____

_____

_____

_____

2. List the godly desires you have in your life.

_____

_____

_____

_____

3. List or think about the ungodly desires that consume your thoughts or guide some of your actions and decisions.

_____

_____

_____

_____

_____

4. What makes you resist God's best for you in those moments when you are stepping toward a temptation or taking a bite of something "forbidden" or unhealthy for you?

_____

_____

_____

_____

_____

5. Memorize Proverbs 4:23: "Keep your heart with all diligence, for out of it spring the issues of life." Write a personal prayer here based on this verse.

_____

_____

_____

_____

_____

6. List three things you can do today to avoid some temptations that are typical for you. Pray over these and ask for God to give you His strength to walk toward life-giving and faith-building choices.

_____

_____

_____

_____

_____

Part Three

Chapter 12

An Apple a Day

Once our eyes are opened to the lies, we are no longer shielded by innocence. And we're certainly not protected by feigning innocence. The truth is out. There's no going back. Think about how many times you've heard a parent correct a child and then say, "You know better than that!" (Maybe you've said it a time or two.)

From this journey and from the fruit of your own experiences, you do know better. You know better than to fall for the lies, to ignore the emotions that rise up during the day, to avoid exploring your heart and avoid the Maker of your heart.

And best of all, you know that a better life awaits the woman who faces the lies with God's strength and claims victory over the deception and the deceiver. This better life is full of purpose, significance, wholeness, and integrity.

This has been a time of growth and personal exploration and vulnerability as you've reviewed your past and present behaviors. The spiritual work that you've done will help you recognize lies that tempt you from this day forward. Because you will likely be faced with at least one "apple" a day, it is important to keep paying attention to the lies that you most often fall for.

The innocence you can claim is the innocence you're given through your salvation. *This* you can live in, hold onto, and stand on. You need this grace because each and every day, you will probably encounter an "apple"—a pretty, disguised invitation to dismiss God's assurances and take a big bite of a lie.

What God Gives You

My father used to take me with him to inspect the fruit trees in our yard. It was one of the highlights of my young life. My father had filled an expanse of our property with an incredible assortment of fruit trees. We had a nectarine tree, an almond tree, two peach trees, four loquat trees, an orange tree, a lemon tree, a fig tree, a banana tree, and a few others I can't remember specifically.

Often Dad would pick one of the tasty fruits and be sure it was ripe and ready to be eaten. Then he would share it with me. I knew it was okay to eat because my father had examined it and extended it to me with love. Those garden walks meant so much to me. From those times of fellowship, I knew that my father cared about me and wanted to nurture our relationship. We shared in the delight of creation and in the delight of our bond.

God wants to come to our garden and walk with us as He did with Adam and Eve. He wants us to get a good feel for the taste of truth. When He walks with us, He points out the fruit growing in our personal gardens and encourages us to delight in it.

Jesus told a parable in Matthew 25 that aptly illustrates this truth. It was about a man who, before traveling to a far country, gave three of his servants talents. To the first servant he gave five talents. To the second servant he gave two talents. To the third servant he gave one talent.

When the man returned from his journey he called his servants in to give an account of what they had done with the talents he had given them. The first servant presented the man with five more talents. The second servant had gained two more talents. However, the third servant had hidden his one talent in the ground. The man commended the first two servants and said to each, "Well done, good and faithful servant; you were faithful over a few things, I will make you ruler over many things. Enter into the joy of your lord" (Matthew 25:21).

> Don't be deceived into thinking that God
> won't make a difference through you.

Sadly, the third servant brought back to the man only the talent he had been given. The master was upset and scolded him.

Then Jesus said, "To everyone who has, more will be given, and he will have abundance; but from him who does not have, even what he has will be taken away" (Matthew 25:29).

Like the servants in the parable, you're called to be a good steward of what you've been given. Your realm to nurture and tend to is your garden. Do you spend time being a good steward, or do you leave things in disarray because you mistakenly see your garden as small and insignificant? Don't be deceived into thinking that God won't make a difference through you. Focus instead on the potential and purpose of your gift of life.

A Life's Harvest

When you've encountered the merciful promises of God, you are compelled to share your faith and watch others grow in truth.

I was told that my grandfather was quite a character. Although I never met him, my father used to tell me stories about him that enthralled me.

My grandfather was raised in a very affluent and secular home. Though he was raised in the church he never imagined the possibility of having a personal relationship with Jesus Christ until later in life.

Before his transformation Grandpa's only daughter was taken ill with spinal meningitis. Grandpa was beside himself. He left for work that day not knowing if his little girl would still be breathing when he returned home.

Returning from work that afternoon, he found his front door wide open. He immediately sensed something was wrong. He ran into the house calling for my grandma and little Ginny, my aunt. The house was empty. A neighbor knocked on the door and told my grandpa that my grandmother had run down the street to the Foursquare pastor's house. She had been carrying her daughter in her arms.

Grandpa rushed down the street and burst into the pastor's house. Entering the house he saw my grandmother on her knees praying. Tears of joy rolled down her radiant face. Grandpa's little daughter, my Aunt Virginia, was sitting straight up conversing gaily with the pastor. Grandpa immediately fell to his knees and began to entreat God to save him. The pastor prayed with Grandpa that day, and he was changed forever!

By the time he encountered the living Savior he had sown quite a few wild oats, burned more than a few bridges, and failed in several endeavors. But when Jesus took over, Grandpa immediately felt God's power in his life. From the time he met Jesus he evangelized everyone he met.

One of his favorite ministries was a once-a-week visit to the local jails. With his Bible held high in his right hand, Grandpa would walk down the corridors of the cell block inviting the prisoners to a Bible study. As he walked he would loudly sing, "There is power, power, power, wonder-working power in the precious blood of the Lamb!" (Grandpa always insisted on adding the extra "power" to the chorus when he sang it.)

So assured of God's forgiveness in his own life, Grandpa couldn't wait to share it with the most hardened criminals. He made sure that every prisoner in every cell knew the effectual power of the blood of Jesus to cleanse every sin and remove it as far as the east is from the west.

Numerous ex-cons ate Sunday dinners at my grandmother's table. My dad remembers many exciting testimonies shared at those meals. Felons, armed robbers, members of the Mafia partook of my grandmother's delicious rolls and savory roasts. They shared their story of redemption with the members of the Smith household while my grandfather interjected, "Hallelujah!"

Grandpa was convinced of the grace of God because he had experienced it firsthand. God had reached out to him while he was still a wretched, self-centered, and temperamental sinner. For the rest of his life this overwhelming sense of God's grace compelled him to convince others of the power of the blood of Jesus Christ to save anyone who would believe.

Grandpa fully embraced the grace that God offered. In response God lavished His grace and power upon my grandpa. My grandfather's garden of life was a place that produced great fruit through his passion to honor a gracious, great God.

What Does Your Garden Look Like?

Your life garden might not be the paradise that Eve initially experienced. There might be more prohibitions in your garden than in hers. You might even have weeds and fruitless trees. However, God has placed you there for a purpose: actually, for your purpose and His purpose. There is a beauty in your garden and you are needed there.

God wants to bring something beautiful out of the very garden that you are in. As you tend to those things He has put into your garden, He will plant even more trees in your garden.

The garden He gives us is the opportunities we have to serve Him. As we serve Him faithfully in whatever He calls us to do, He will increase our garden and bless its fruit.

Are you a mother? Then what a beautiful garden you have! Psalm 128:3 describes children as "like olive plants all around your table." As you tend to your children, praying for them, nourishing them, tending to their needs, and teaching them the wonderful truths of God's Word, you will see your garden blossom and become an oasis of beauty, peace, and security.

Are you single? What an opportunity you have to minister to others! You can invite and plant all sorts of beautiful things in your garden. You have the freedom to travel to different gardens and bring the seedlings of their fruitful trees to your own.

Do you work? Then your job can be your garden. You can pray for the other employees. You can ask God for ways to help and encourage those around you. A friend of ours worked in a very secular environment. Every day before he left for work, he and his wife would get on their knees and pray for the people in his office. Before he left his house he would call out to his wife, "I'm on my way to my mission field."

What trees are in your garden? Do you cook? Do you clean? Do you have a gift for organizing? Do you love to teach? Do you sew? Do you sing? Look around you and inside you to notice all the amazing opportunities and blessings God has entrusted to you.

Let All the Lies Go—Watch Your Garden Grow

The day your heart releases its hold on the lies is the day you become open to a fruitful and faithful life. Hopefully, along this path, you've gathered different tools to help you resist the enticing falsehoods and the unhealthy, ungodly beliefs that keep you doubting God's love and promises. To keep you moving forward, I want to encourage you to participate in practices that will strengthen your resolve to walk in truth. Make these a part of your daily life so that you choose to say no when a shiny false fruit tempts you to discount God's Word and His plan for you.

Talk to God

Strengthen your resistance by praying to God. When Satan enters your thoughts, turn your thoughts to prayer. Invite God into all your meditations. David prayed, "Give ear to my words, O LORD, consider my meditation" (Psalm 5:1). I find that when I invite the Lord into my meditations, Satan flees.

So consider turning your thoughts into conversations with the Lord. The Bible encourages us to "pray without ceasing" and promises us that God will work in our circumstances if we will pray. So develop your prayer life.

I have a friend who never lets me off the phone without praying. It has become a habit for her. She prays for everyone who calls her. I can't think of a better habit to develop than prayer. It yields benefits today and great rewards for tomorrow.

Dwell on God's Word

Read your Bible daily. Even if you can only get a portion in, read and think about what you have read. I like to keep a journal handy when I read. I try to write down at least one thought from God's Word that I want to stay with me that day. In this way, I am not just reading but thinking about God's Word all through the day.

Another way to let God's Word shape your life and your thoughts is to read slowly through the Gospels. There are times when I like to take each story in the Gospels all by itself. Rather than reading a whole chapter or through chapters, I will read only the portion dealing with Jesus cleansing a leper, going to Jairus's house, feeding the multitude, or addressing the multitudes from the shore of Galilee. In my notes I paraphrase the story, putting it into my own words. Then I think about it all day.

Praise the Lord

Worship the Lord in songs and hymns. Christian music contains some of the most uplifting truths about God. Music has a way of playing over and over again in our minds and working its way into our hearts.

I came across a new term last year when I was reading a periodical. It talked about *earworms*. It described earworms as those songs that get stuck in your head and can't get out. I've had quite a few of those. When I find myself humming some lame tune from the 1970s, I like to replace it with a Christian song. Sometimes I play a CD of Christian songs while driving. I'll turn it up and sing along. Yes, I know how it looks to the people in other cars, but I'm simply not bothered about what they think. I need to worship!

Colossians 3:16 instructs us to "let the word of Christ dwell in you richly in all wisdom, teaching and admonishing one another in psalms and hymns and spiritual songs, singing with grace in your hearts to the Lord."

Worship the Lord! I think the enemy flees when he hears the truth of God's Word being belted out in song.

Delight in God's Character

We delight in the Lord by making Him our priority and our first consideration. We take our mind off an unhealthy desire and endeavor to dwell on the attributes of God. I find it very enlightening and comforting to make lists of His attributes. It can be ones that come to my mind, or ones that are brought out during the reading of Scripture. Looking at the many ways I experience His faithful character leads me to deep thanksgiving.

A friend of mine carries a spiral-bound notebook of special scriptures that the Lord has given to her during times in her life when she needed His loving Word and guidance. Whenever she is tempted by a wrong desire, she flips through her notebook reminding herself of God's goodness and promises.

Celebrate Faith Stories

A wonderful way to infuse your heart and soul with the good news of God's transforming love is to listen to the testimony of other believers and to reflect on your own story. God is doing amazing things in people's lives. Are you being a witness of the miracles happening every day?

I love to read missionary biographies for a dose of inspiration. God works through ordinary lives to do extraordinary things. Don't miss out on the chance to see God's purpose unfolding. It is happening all around you and *in* you.

Beyond the Lies

Imagine the scene in the house of Martha in Bethany. While she busied herself with much serving, her sister, Mary, sat at Jesus' feet listening to Him. Martha, feeling isolated and angry with her sister, accusingly approached Jesus, "Lord, do You not care that my sister has left me to serve alone?" (Luke 10:40).

Martha took it as a personal affront that Jesus would allow Mary to sit at His feet while she worked single-handedly to prepare the necessities to serve Him. In hyperfocusing on the workload, Martha was vulnerable to the devil's lie that Jesus didn't care about her.

> Don't let *anything* become more important than being
> in the presence of the Lord. Each day is a chance
> to experience all that God has for you.

Jesus had come to Martha's home. He was sitting in her house. He was speaking. Yet, Martha was missing the love, the joy, and the fellowship of the Son of God because of her single focus on duty. If she would have taken inventory of all God had given her, she would have shared the glory with her sister in sitting at the feet of Jesus.

Jesus addressed her, "Martha, Martha..." I love the way He said her name twice. I think the first time didn't count. Martha was pretty worked up by this time. She had built quite a case for herself and was wrapped up in self-pity. I think the first "Martha" was to interrupt her thoughts and the second "Martha" was to get her attention.

Having gotten Martha's attention, Jesus corrected her: "You are worried and troubled about many things. But one thing is needed, and Mary has chosen that good part, which will not be taken away from her" (Luke 10:41-42). While Martha was building a case of self-pity, Mary was enjoying the blessing of sitting in the presence of Jesus.

Don't let *anything* become more important than being in the presence of the Lord. Each day is a chance to experience all that God has for you. Become a woman who sees beyond the lies, my friend. "Blessed is she who has believed that the Lord would fulfill his promises to her!" (Luke 1:45 NIV). The verity of God's love, mercy, faithfulness, and hope is yours to hold forever.

Questions for Study and Personal Reflection

1. Living a better life for God is an exciting adventure. What specific truths are helping you walk with God and walk toward a life of purpose?

_____

_____

_____

_____

2. What will you do when you encounter an "apple a day"? How are you prepared for temptation?

_____

_____

_____

_____

3. What has God entrusted to you? What is your garden?

_____

_____

_____

4. What do you hope will be your life's harvest? How are you seeing this unfolding now?

_____

_____

_____

_____

5. In what ways is your life changing since you began letting go
   of lies?

_____

_____

_____

_____

6. Memorize this verse: "Blessed is she who has believed that the
   Lord would fulfill his promises to her!" (Luke 1:45 NIV). What
   does this mean to you? What promises give you great hope as
   you live in God's truths?

_____

_____

_____

_____

Embracing Truth Journal

We are at end of our adventure together, but I want to encourage you to keep recognizing any falsehoods that appear in your life. I pray that now you will know how to live in the fullness of God's beautiful truth and mercy. The more you recognize your weaknesses, the better able you will be to recognize His power. The more willing you are to let go of deceptions, the more able you are to hold onto His promises.

Keep up the good work that you have started. The following journal pages are to help you continue. Make copies of them and record your insights and prayers for as long as the Lord leads you to, so that you can pursue this ongoing faith-strengthening activity.

Embracing Truth Journal

Day _____

What lie are you facing today?

_____

_____

_____

Talk to God. Write out a prayer for guidance.

_____

_____

_____

_____

_____

Dwell on God's Word. Select and write out a verse that speaks to you. Underline the words that stand out to you.

_____

_____

_____

_____

_____

Praise the Lord. List five things you are grateful for. Give God thanksgiving.

- _____

- _____

- _____

- _____

- _____

Delight in God's character. What aspect of God's nature are you resting in?

_____

_____

_____

Celebrate your faith story. How is your garden growing? How is God moving in your life?

_____

_____

_____

What truth will you embrace today?

_____

_____

_____

About the Author

Cheryl Brodersen has been serving Jesus together with her husband, Brian, for over 30 years. The Brodersens have four grown children and four adorable grandsons. Cheryl is the daughter of Pastor Chuck Smith of Calvary Chapel Costa Mesa and his beautiful wife, Kay.

Cheryl currently teaches the Friday morning women's Bible study at Calvary Chapel Costa Mesa and hosts the show *Today's Faith*, seen on HisChannel.com. She has taught women's classes at the Calvary Chapel Bible College in addition to teaching seminars, lecturing, and sharing at women's conferences and retreats.

Cheryl's passion for Jesus and His Word are evident when she speaks. Her enthusiasm for things of God is infectious.

Visit Cheryl at
www.facebook.com/CherylBrodersen
www.graciouswords.com

See Cheryl on
Today's Faith at www.HisChannel.com

When a Woman Lets Go of Her Fears
The Amazing Power of Trusting God
Cheryl Brodersen

Fear in a woman's life can be controlling, deceptive, and downright crippling. You want to be free but just can't see how it can happen.

But there's help. Cheryl Brodersen, speaker, author, and teacher, knows anxiety firsthand. She reveals her fears, the struggle to escape them, and how she finally broke the chains fear had wrapped around her heart and mind. Her practical insights help you...

- let go of fear's familiarity and trust God
- eliminate the "what if" fears
- use the faith you already have to fight fear

Like Cheryl, you can begin to listen to God through His Word even in the midst of your pain. You can take the first steps on a beautiful journey toward freedom...finding peace and confidence in God.

Growing Together As a Couple
10 Biblical Essentials for Building a Great Marriage
Brian and Cheryl Brodersen

God designed marriage to draw husbands and wives closer to one another and to His love. Are you experiencing the wholeness and joy of a marriage nurtured spiritually, physically, and emotionally?

With honesty about their moments of growing apart and their moments of awakening to God's plan, the Brodersens share ten godly essentials to help you...

- *entrust* your relationship to God
- *eliminate* unhealthy expectations
- *enlighten* with spiritual truth
- *energize* the relationship
- *endure* by standing together in faith

This biblical wisdom and encouraging guidance will lead you to embrace the very best human love experience possible—just as God intended.

The Confident Woman
Knowing Who You Are in Christ
Anabel Gillham

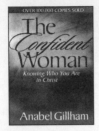

Do you struggle to be the "perfect Christian" for God, your family, your employer, your friends? You're not alone.

But God doesn't call you to be "perfect." He calls you to be *confident*—because of His love, His acceptance, and the life of His Son, Jesus, inside you. Anabel Gillham shares with you God's plan for freedom, rest, and peace, showing you from Scripture what a truly confident woman looks like.

One-Minute Prayers™ for Young Women
Hope Lyda

"This book is a great way for you to start a conversation with God and begin a lasting, intimate relationship with your Creator."

—Robin Marsh and Lauren Nelson,
authors of *God, Girls, and Getting Connected*

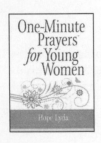

You have a lot going on—expectations and possibilities, friendships and new relationships, growth and change. These short prayers will help you connect with the God who cares about you and knows what your heart needs.

God made you unique and filled you with ideas and dreams and abilities. Talk to Him—He can't wait to listen to you and to share in your life.

Today, like every day, You invite me
to be a part of Your purpose and compassion for the world.
God, thanks for including me! Amen.

The Power of a Woman's Words

Sharon Jaynes

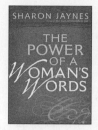

Your words become the mirror in which others see themselves. Words are one of the most significant forces in the universe, and they can be used for good or evil. Your words can change the course of a day...the course of a life. Popular speaker Sharon Jaynes will help you use your words in positive, powerful ways, so that you can...

- instill confidence into a child's heart
- encourage a husband to accomplish his dreams
- fan the dying embers of a friend's smoldering hope
- draw someone to the love of Christ

As a woman, you can explore the power you possess, the people you impact, the potential for change, and the profound possibilites as you harness this mighty force and use it to speak life to those around you.

Beautiful Battle

A Woman's Guide to Spiritual Warfare

Mary DeMuth

Warfare. Hell. Demons. I'm just trying to drive my kids to school and stay on top of the laundry. What does any of that have to do with me?

With passion and strength, Mary DeMuth brings balance and insight to the often murky realm of spiritual warfare. As you embrace the abundant life to which God calls His daughters, she'll tell you why your voice matters for eternity.

And on the darkest days, you'll know that spiritual warfare is about bowing before the Creator, not cowering before the devil. It's about finding freedom and beauty in the midst of devastation. It's about the power of God to heal our hearts, to move mountains, to intercede when we're weary. It's about crucifixion and a defiant, glorious resurrection.

It's about truth. It's about power. Join Mary in the beautiful battle, and be renewed on the journey.